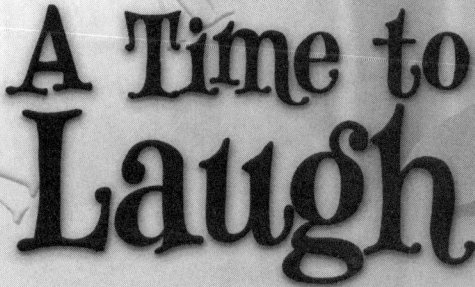

A Time to Laugh

A TIME TO LISTEN

Thoughts that open the heart and stir the soul through simchah

RABBI YEHOSHUA KURLAND

A Time to Laugh

ISRAEL BOOKSHOP
PUBLICATIONS

Thoughts that open the heart and stir the soul through simchah

A TIME TO LISTEN

Rabbi Yehoshua Kurland

Copyright © 2009 by Rabbi Yehoshua Kurland

978-1-60091-103-3

All Rights Reserved

No part of this book may be reproduced in any form
without written permission from the copyright holder.
The Rights of the Copyright Holder Will Be Strictly Enforced

Book & Cover design by:

SRULY PERL • 845.694.7186

Distributed by:

Israel Bookshop Publications

 501 Prospect Street
Lakewood, NJ 08701
Tel: (732) 901-3009
Fax: (732) 901-4012
www.israelbookshoppublications.com
info@israelbookshoppublications.com

Printed in the USA

Dedication

This book is dedicated to the loving memory
of my dear parents and in-laws

Rabbi Yaakov and
Rebbetzin Miriam Kurland *z"l*

and

Yisroel and **Dena Zelman** *z"l*

לעילוי נשמות הורינו היקרים

הרב **חזקיהו יעקב** ב"ר **בנימין** ז"ל
והרבנית **מרים** בת הרב **יעקב אריה הלוי** ז"ל
קורלאנד

ר' **ישראל** ב"ר **ישעיה משולם זיסל** ז"ל
ומרת **דינה** בת ר' **יהודה** ז"ל
זלמן

No words can possibly express our profound *hakaras
hatov* to have been *zocheh* to such wonderful parents.

ת. נ. צ. ב. ה.

In loving memory of

אביבה יוכבד בת מנחם מענדל ע"ה

Mrs. Aviva Ghatan ע"ה

In loving memory of

ר׳ **משה אהרן** בן ר׳ **אברהם** ע״ה

and

זיסל בת ר׳ **ישעיה הערץ** ע״ה

Mr. and Mrs. **Monroe Fragin** ע״ה

Two gentle *neshamos* who personified the radiance and sunshine that a human being can infuse into another, with a smile and a good word. Their "*simchas hachaim*" was an inspiration to all.

ת.נ.צ.ב.ה.

In loving memory of our dear son

חיים שמואל בן ר׳ **יחזקאל יהושע** ע״ה

ת.נ.צ.ב.ה.

Naomi and Charles Steinberg

לעילוי נשמות הורינו היקרים

ר׳ **יצחק** ב״ר **משה** ע״ה

ומרת **חנה** בת ר׳ **חיים** ע״ה העכנער

ור׳ **יעקב מרדכי** ב״ר **חנוך טוביה** ע״ה ס״ט

ת.נ.צ.ב.ה.

Table of Contents

- **Introduction: A Time to Laugh; A Time to Listen** — 31
- **Between Man and G-d**
    - Fear of Heaven: It's Yours for the Asking (Yearning for *yiras shamayim*) — 39
    - Has Anyone Seen My Father? (The legacy of Yaakov Avinu) — 43
    - I Don't Even Know You (*"V'habotai'ach baHashem chessed yisovivenu"*) — 48
    - It Ain't Just Luck (Accruing *zechuyos*) — 53
    - Sing His Praises O' You Nations (The Hidden Salvation) — 57
- **Between Man and Himself**
    - Oblivious (*Ein adam ro'eh nigei atzmo*) — 63
    - Priorities (Relinquishing one's heart) — 66
    - What's In a Name? (Finding one's *shoresh haneshamah*) — 70
- **Between Man and His Fellow Man**
    - Everybody Counts - I Don't Get No Respect (Looking at the potential) — 77
    - Giving, Never Taking (*"A gut morgen, a gut yahr"*) — 81

Emissaries of Hashem (Giving is all gain)	88
Happy with His Portion ("This above all else, to thy own self be true")	91
Invisible (I feel your weight)	95
Selflessness (The great prize of being a *"ma'avir al midosav"*)	99
That's His Problem (The staunch *emunah* of the *oseik bitzarchei tzibur*)	104
We'll Leave the Light on for You (Giving life to others)	108

■ Festivals

Elul: Teshuvah - How Will I Ever Get There? (A small step for man, a huge step for mankind)	115
Rosh Hashanah: Teshuvah - Return to Your Essence (Connecting to the G-dliness within)	118
Shabbos Shuvah: You Make Your Own Lunch (Yes you can! It's up to you!)	123
Yom Kippur: Teshuvah - Coming Home (Rejoining the ranks of the *"mamleches kohanim v'goy kadosh"*)	129
Yom Kippur: Neilah: Teshuvah - Help Me Stop Stealing (Actualizing our full potential)	133
Sukkos: It's Time to Go Home (Under the shade and the protection of The One Above)	137
Chanukah: Instant *Kedushah* (*Kedushah* is attainable but not instantaneous)	141
Purim: Everyone Should Enjoy Purim (The joy of basking in "His" glory)	145
Pesach: Freedom of Religion (The freedom to actualize our *kochos haneshamah*)	151
Shavuos: Wheelbarrows (The ikkur is the keili)	156

Tisha B'av: Tears Of Hope - Turn A Tear Into A Prayer   159
(The crying of a Jew is one of hopefulness)

■ Internal Struggles

Compartmentalization: Light And Darkness All in One   167
(The aggregate conflict in one man)

Enemies in the West (Dealing with Eisav when he acts as your brother)   172

Here Today Gone Tomorrow (Becoming an accomplice to the *Yetzer Hara*)   176

Who Is Like You, Hashem? (You even sustain the rebel)   180

■ Spiritual Tools

Man's True Strength (Uniting the forces of one's heart)   187

Not So Fast (The pros and cons of adaptation)   191

To Tell the Truth (Unflinching commitment to integrity)   197

■ Shalom Bayis - The Home

Home Sweet Home (*Midos tovos* and *eidelkeit* begin at home)   205

Sailing the Seven C's of *Chinuch* (Seven rules to follow in *chinuch habanim*)   209

The Bar Mitzvah - The *Bar Chiyuvah* (The privilege of serving the Master and adhering to His decrees)   217

■ Tefilah

Keep on Shuckling (*"Kavei el Hashem chazak v'ya'ameitz libechah v'kavei el Hashem"*)   225

Tefillah: It's Not Just Three Times a Day (*Tefillah- chayei sha'ah -* 24/7)   230

- **The World We Live In**

    Deadheads (The precious moments of real living)   237

    Life Insurance (The secret to longevity)   241

- **Torah**

    Never the Same: The Same Thing Syndrome (Real learning - constant review)   247

    The "*Chein*" of the Plain and the Humble ("*Ul'anovim yitein chein*")   252

    Turn a *Shiur* Into a Prayer (*Limud haTorah*; an exercise in *d'veikus*)   257

- **Sources and Outlines**   261

- **Glossary**   297

בס״ד

אגרת ברכה

הן גילה אני נגיל בעצם
כי יום פקדני... כ׳ אדר תשע״ט

חביבא אתי תלמידי כבני... כבקשתו אמרתי לדבר ולענות לפני גדולה "הגדול" (שמואל ואן) כה
אמר. שלמי היה כסדר הזה... לדבר יום... ש'אין הימים תערוך לימי ילדות רבה: ואמריך לכן ולנו
ולנו ועתליין פרט לבחורים בפני הנערך ו'מקים ולבן" (אבות ה) רבי אליא דאמר. כינס
ש'בים בן גער ויורד מלה׳ בחורים שהנערך ופועל על אדם לעברו ולחטו'ל ערב לחם
פרט אמן לבקש כן בגגר ילד מלה׳ בכונס לאדם בשים מצוה שיצא בשערי תפילה
ועולה ברוב ולמב בן מלה׳ בבחורים אדם קונץ לו הרי רבי ואתן אמר השמים
בהינך לידע ל"ז (לאבות ה") לי הא דרבת עלי בעמת אילו רבי את נלמד סתחולים ולמרי רבב

[...שורות נוספות...]

הכותב למנוע לבהל הנסיה ואהבה נפשנית

RAV SHMUEL BRAZIL
1133 SAGE ST. FAR ROCKAWAY, N.Y. 11691

בס״ד

י״ב מנחם אב תשס״ט

לכבוד ידידי היקר עד מאד משפיע ומרביץ תורה לרבים מוה״ר ר' יהושע נ״י

You have always been an inspirer of all ages, both men and women alike, facilitating their *Aliyah* in Torah and *Yiddishkeit* by using your געבענטש *chochmas haTorah*, warmth, and wit and sense of humor. Over the years working together as Rabbeim in Yeshivas Shor Yoshuv, I have constantly witnessed how your unique, engaging style and incredible demonstrative love for *Yidden*, nourished them to grow and to actualize their potential in becoming true *B'nei Torah* and *Ehrliche Baalei Batim* who are seriously *kovaiyah eetim* for *limud haTorah*. Hashem has given you a remarkable talent that during the same *Derasha*, you have literally caused your audience to shed tears through a heart rendering and riveting story or passionate point, soon to be followed by tears that flow from an uncontrollable laughter, having been embraced by your poignant humor together with your flawless delivery.

For making people happy and lifting up their spirits alone, one receives unfathomable *s'char* in Olam Habbah. We were both *zocheh* to hear our great Rebbe, Reb Shlomo *zt"l* relate on numerous occasions the Gemarah in *Taanis* that extols the virtues of the "two clowns," dubbing them "בני עלמא דאתי". However, when the humor is immediately followed by a message and a *Mussar*, then the reward is twofold. It is through the medium of Simcha that even the most stubborn heart can be pried open and is transformed into a receptacle to receive the *Mussar*, consequently inspiring the listener to committing in making a meaningful change in his life.

The Gemarah says that there are two ways to acquire an object: through lifting and through pulling (הגבהה and משיכה). Lifting is the superior method of acquisition. The *Middah* of *simchah* has the ability to lift off of one's heart all the heaviness, pressures, and disappointments that incessantly obstruct the entry of thoughts that motivate a spiritual awakening. However, once that burden is relieved, and one's Lev is accessible, penetrable, and open to listen, the Yid can acquire a *Yeshuah* by following a path toward self-improvement.

It is brought down that the author of a *sefer* should hint his name in its title. Rav Yehoshua (Heshel) Simcha, you need not bother since the entire contents of your *sefer* from beginning to end totally embodies your name. It is my humble *brachah* to you that each inspiring message and theme should bring about personal spiritual *yeshuos* and change in the lives of the readers through the powerful medium of *simchah*.

בידידות רבה בלב ונפש
שמואל ברזל

בברכה שתצליח לעורר לבות בנ״י לאביהם שבשמים

RABBI JOSEPH ROTTENBERG
3301 B TANEY ROAD
BALTIMORE MD 21215
410 578-8245

הרב יוסף נחמן ראטטענבערג
ראש ישיבת חפץ חיים
באלטימאר

בע"ה יום ג' פ' לך לך הבעל"ט לפ"ק

אהובי ידידי הרה"ח מוה"ר אלעזר שליט"א הנזכר לעיל אני שמח מאד בהצלחתן וכו' וקבלתי את מכתבן ידידי. הרבה לדבר אין לי אבל תדע נאמנה ונאמנה לידידנו שליט"א אשר שוקיקים לראותן ואבקש ויבקש אצל הקב"ה בן שיכולנו לראות פנים פה להתראות בשלום לאורך ימים טובים ואמן.

לאשר נשאל ממני את דעתי על ידידנו כל ידידותינו בקשתם מלא הם ותמיד הוא ידידי ע"י הישיבה בפאלם ביטש שמה ובא לא לכתי אמר שילא כדרכו ויכוא יעקב ולך דטון יבדר הישיבה ולצר ישא.

ואודיעני על כל הנעשה כסף נא יגיע אודיעני. ועוד דבר שיודעני נוח לנו עם ייתכן שצי לרב דלא יסבול כדוגלנו על כל הקונוסים ואצלי חתמלא הענין ויה' לעד בנכון ה' אקוה

פה"ק יוסף נחמן ראטטענבערג

Acknowledgements

הודו לה' כי טוב כי לעולם חסדו...

All gratitude and appreciation must begin and end with the unequivocal recognition of the gift of life that *Hakadosh Baruch Hu* so graciously bestows upon us every second. As we stand to daven *Shemoneh Esrei,* we begin by uttering those humbling words, "*Hashem s'fasai tiftach* - Hashem, open my lips and allow my mouth to declare Your praise." *Ribono Shel Olam*, my sole ability to pray and plead before You for my very life is due to Your unending kindness. That my mind can conjure up thoughts, that my throat, my palate, my tongue, my teeth, and my lips can utter sounds, that those sounds can somehow form words and thereby convey and articulate ideas, is only because You permit me the privilege. I dare not begin my *tefillah* without first declaring this *hakarah* with the greatest of *shevach vehoda'ah* to the *Borei niv s'fasayim* - the creator of the utterances of the lips, the Master of the universe. And I dare not attempt to issue these essays without expressing my unceasing *hakaras hatov* to Hashem for enabling me to commit my thoughts to the written word, with the sincere hope that the words that flow from my heart, will enter the heart of the reader, and will serve as a source of inspiration and engender personal growth.

In preparing this book, one prevailing thought that continues to permeate my mind is: who am I to impose my modified understanding of the holy teachings of *Chazal* and the great *baalei avodah*, as well as my worthy *rebbeim*, to a reading public? Nonetheless, I throw my hat into the ring, with the hope that the *Ribono Shel Olam* has guided me on a path that is true and authentic. I thank my many *talmidim* over the last thirty six years, and audiences who were present at various speaking engagements in the past, for serving as the victims in allowing me the opportunity to attempt to clarify in my own mind, the *hargashos*, sensations of my heart, and the spirit of my soul. I assume sole responsibility for any misunderstanding or misrepresentation of information or the interpretation thereof. I pray that the meditations of my heart are clearly echoed in these pages in an orderly fashion that will prove to be a source of inspiration and practical application. The inclusion of a humorous story introducing each segment is intended to induce a bit of laughter to facilitate a more attentive and relaxed reader. This is with the hope that once a rapport is established through the universal language of humor, the reader will allow himself to expand into a formidable vessel for the maximum absorption of the subject matter in the spirit of the classic *milsa d'bedichusa*, opening joke, mentioned in the Talmud.

This volume is dedicated to the memory of my dearly departed parents and in-laws, Rabbi Yaakov and Miriam Kurland and R' Yisrael and Dena Zelman *z"l*. The impact they made on our lives and the lives of others cannot be measured in words. They made an otherwise difficult-to-fulfill *vort* of the famed Mirrer *rosh yeshiva* Harav Chaim Shmulevitz *zt"l* more true-to-life and pragmatic. Rav Chaim writes in the *Sichos Mussar* that in order to properly fulfill the *mitzvah* of *kibud av va'eim*, one needs to find in each of one's parents an attribute or inclination that he excels in, that would render him a *gadol hador* in those areas of behavior. Anything less fails to capture the optimal fulfillment of this *mitzvah*. This task, daunting as it may be, was a simple matter in regard to our parents. From my father's unusual *chavivus haTorah* and loveable and unassuming nature, to my mother's natural warmth and unconditional love and belief in all people; from my father-in-law's super-human pleasant demeanor, *emuneh peshutah*, and perspicacity, to my mother-in-law's humility and total *hisbatlus* to the will of others and most assuredly the *ratzon* Hashem, there was much to emulate and hold in high regard. It is with much *hakaras hatov* to the *Ribono Shel Olam* for granting us the privilege to have had such greatness at our side, guiding and supporting our every move, that I dedicate this book to their memory. No doubt, the humorous stories of this volume would have brought a smile to such people who personified a life filled with a *simchas hachaim*; but more importantly, the lessons to be learned would have justifiably served as a testimony to the way they lived their lives. May they merit a *lichtigah Gan Eiden* as those who brought an abundance of light to the beautiful worlds that they built on this earth. *Yehei zichram baruch.*

How does one thank his *rebbeim*, when their input is monumental and eternal? *Baruch Hashem*, I was *zocheh* to learn from and observe *emesdikah talmidei chachamim* in every sense of the word. My *rebbeim* in Yeshivas Chafetz Chaim of Baltimore, the *rosh hayeshiva*, Harav Chaim Samson *zt"l*, the *mashgiach*, Harav Boruch Milikowski *zt"l*, and the *menahel* and principal, Dr. Gershon Kranzler *zt"l* were all exceptional *talmidei chachamim* and *mechanchim par excellence* who taught both through example and deed.

To my *rebbe, rosh hayeshivah* of Yeshivas Chafetz Chaim of Baltimore, Harav Yosef Rottenberg *shlit"a*, I have no words that can adequately convey my feelings of thankfulness for all that he has done for me as a *rebbi*, a mentor, a *poseik*, a *baal miyaeitz*, and as one who has offered only encouragement and tremendous *chizuk* to myself and all of his hundreds of *talmidim* who love him as a father. *Rebbe*, your great warmth and humor and earnest and nonjudgmental acceptance of every *talmid* with love and absolute belief in his potential, has taught me volumes in how a *rebbi* should view a *talmid*. To be such a *talmid chacham muflag*, and yet to possess the genius to make every person who is *zocheh* to sit in your *dalet amos* feel like an equal, is a talent that I will always emulate. May you have a *refuah sheleimah bisoch shaar cholei Yisrael* and be *zocheh* together with your wonderful *rebbetzin* to many years together in good health until a hundred and twenty years.

I had the *zechus* to learn in Yeshivah Kol Torah in Bayit Vegan, a noble *makom torah* under the guidance of the *rosh hayeshiva*, Harav Moshe Yehudah Schlessinger *shlit"a*. There, I had the *zechus* to bask in the glory of the presence of its *rosh hayeshivah*, Harav Shlomo Zalman Auerbach *zt"l*, and *yibadel l'chaim tovim*, the *mashgiach*, Harav Gedalya Eisemann *shlit"a*. It afforded me the privilege to see such Torah giants as Harav Elya Lopian *zt"l* and Harav Yechezkiel Abrambsky *zt"l*. My *rebbeim*, the Rosh Yeshiva Harav Elchonon Kunstdat *zt"l*, Harav Shmuel Steinhaus *zt"l* and *yibadel l'chaim tovim* Harav Yehoshua Neuvirth *shlit"a* made an indelible impression upon me. The Yeshivah is true to its name, as the reverberations of the sweet *kol torah* that resonate from the windows of its *beis medrash*, still echo in my ears.

Yeshivas Ner Yisrael had a prominent influence upon our family as we grew up in Baltimore, for it had been my father's *zt"l* home for close to ten years where he developed a close relationship with its venerable *rosh hayeshivah*, Harav Yaakov Yitzchok Halevi Ruderman *zt"l*, from whom he received his *semichah*. To simply hear my father speak so lovingly about "Rebbi" was a penetrating lesson in and of itself. I too had the privilege to learn in the *yeshivah*, where I was *zocheh* to hear the symphonic *shiurim* of my *Rebbe*, later to become *rosh hayeshivah*, Harav Yaakov Moshe Kulefsky *zt"l*, a prince of a person, and to witness his legendary and awe-inspiring *chavivus hatorah* on a daily basis. To sit in the same *beis medrash* as Harav Ruderman *zt"l* and the *mashgiach*, Harav Dovid Kronglass *zt"l* is a memory that lasts for a lifetime.

Expressing *hakaras hatov* to Yeshivas Shor Yoshuv is an impossible task. It has been my home for the past thirty-eight years and the mainstay of our *mishpachah*. It has afforded me the opportunity to bask in the oasis of a *beis hamedrash* and to engage in the most gainful and fulfilling employment that could possibly exist, that of teaching Torah and attempting to imbue *talmidim*. It has allowed me to connect to various *kiruv* organizations, *yeshivos,* seminaries, and *shuls* to extend my efforts to try to be *marbitz Torah* in that venue. It has opened our home to the *bnei hayeshivah* for *seudos* Shabbos and *Yom Tov* and *sheva brachos, siyumim* and *misibos, shabatonim, shiurim*, and our summer learning program(*Machaneh L'chaim*), as well as our weekly *shalosh seudos* for the *bachurim* of the yeshivah. It has been a source of strength and inspiration for my wife and myself and my children from which we have been the fortunate recipients.

Words are inadequate to capture the deep-seated appreciation, love and, reverence that I feel for the founder and *rosh hayeshivah* of Yeshivas Shor Yoshuv, *Mori Harav* Rabbi Shlomo Freifeld *zt"l*. Affectionally referred to as "the *Rebbe*" by his many *talmidim*, he was a unique *talmid chacham*, who was a fascinating blend of passion and fervor, sagacity and judiciousness, cloaked in an imposing physical presence that housed a heart filled with love and respect for his fellow human being and an absolute belief in their potential. He was an idealist, yet a pragmatist, who had the uncanny genius to find the equilibrium that would elicit and awaken the yearning and the pining of the Jewish soul to reach and stretch to fulfill its potential. His *ahavas Yisrael* was contagious, his love for *talmidei chachamim* exuberant, his love for the *Ribono Shel Olam* ebullient and overflowing. He taught us about the power of *ratzon*, about the *tzuras ha'adam*, about the symmetry of Hashem's world and the crucial role every *Yid* plays in Hashem's master orchestration. He taught us how to discern between *kodesh* and *chol*, between *ohr* and *choshech*, and between Klal Yisrael and the nations of the world, with a depth of understanding that provoked an *azus d'kedushah* that allowed one's *neshamah* full expression. All of this and much more was accomplished by establishing an immediate rapport through his genuine warmth and humor and a down to earth naturalness that penetrated and broke all barriers. Many of the ideas expressed in this volume are manifestations of the twenty years that I was *zocheh* to be in the *dalet amos* of this *gadol b'yisrael,* for which I am eternally grateful.

During my early years in Shor Yoshuv, I had the *zechus* to learn from eminent *talmidei chachamim* who served as the *magidei shiur* at that time. To my *rebbi* of many years Harav Yosef Rabinowitz *shlit"a* I cannot thank him enough for affording me the privilege to hear his inspiring *shiurim* and for the many hours spent with me *b'chavrusah*. May he continue to inspire his *talmidim* and *mispallelim* with his genuine love of Torah through his *gadlus baTorah,* in good health, until a hundred and twenty. I thank Harav Binyamin Forst *shlit"a*, Harav Moshe Chaim Hunger *shlit"a*, Harav Chaim Septimus *shlit"a*, and Harav Refael Weingot *shlit"a*, in addition to my dear friend Harav Moshe Dov Stein *zt"l,* for serving as wonderful role models and sharing their wealth of knowledge and erudition.

To the present-day *rosh hayeshivah* of Yeshivas Shor Yoshuv, *yedidi hane'eman v'hayakar; yedid nafshi,* Harav Naftali Jaeger *shlit"a:* I wish to express my deepest *hakaras hatov* and heartfelt gratitude for his inspirational leadership of our *beis medrash* and *kehilah* as well as his magnanimous personal friendship as a *chaver tov* and confidant. From the earlier years of sharing our dreams for the *yeshivah*, to the exalted *beis medrash* as it stands today; from the many years when the *rosh hayeshiva* was kind enough to learn with me second *seder*, to our numerous trips together to Eretz Yisrael to recruit, the privilege to enjoy a close relationship with such an *Oisge'arbetah talmid chacham* is most cherished and dear to my heart. His *gadlus baTorah* is so beautifully blended with a natural humility that endears him to all. The unusual *chavivus haTorah* and immeasurable *ameilus baTorah* of the *Rosh Hayeshivah*, the *amkus* and the uncanny ability to descend to the essence of a matter, acquiring every step on the way, has had a profound influence on myself and thousands of *talmidim*. As I once remarked at a *yeshivah* alumni reunion, adapting from the words of the great Manchester Rav *zt"l*, "The *rosh hayeshivah* doesn't simply learn the Tosfos, the *rosh hayeshivah* loves the Tosfos!" That *ruach* of his *ahavas haTorah* has pervaded the four walls of our *beis medrash* as *baruch Hashem* there exists a continual flow of learning from four in the morning to the wee hours of the night. With a heart full of *hakaras Hatov*, I thank the *rosh hayeshiva* for allowing me to be part of such a unique *makom Torah* and share in the glorious past, present, and very bright future of perhaps the most unique *makom Torah* in the entire world, Yeshivas Shor Yoshuv. May he and his Rebbetzin be zocheh to lead our *yeshivah* and *kehilah, ad bias go'el tzedek*.

No Yeshiva could function without the *mesiras nefesh* of the *yechidei segulah*, the selfless and self-sacrificing *baalei achrayos*, who are willing to take upon their shoulders the weight of inflationary budgets out of control. It means sleepless nights and deadlines, not to mention the *bizyonos* that often accompanies knocking on doors. To assume such responsibility in addition to a myriad of unrelated *chessed* activity with such dignity, demands a unique and noble individual, dedicated and devoted to the *Ribono Shel Olam's* call. My close friend, Rav Avraham Halpern *shlit"a*, the *menahel* of Yeshivas Shor Yoshuv, is such a person, and I want to express my profound appreciation for all that he does both professionally and as a close personal friend whose genuine care and concern is always felt.

Harav Shmuel Brazil *shlit"a* has literally inspired the Torah world with his *hartzigeh nigunim,* uplifting *sefarim,* and novel *shiurim*. A *baal Regesh* par excellence, I am proud to call him my *chaver tov* and close acquaintance. In particular, I want to thank Rav Shmuel for encouraging me to embark on this project from the beginning, and for reviewing many of the manuscripts. Your *chizuk* in this regard and always, has been a great source of strength for me personally and I thank you with a deep sense of affection. May Hashem bless your new endeavor in Eretz Yisrael with a *shefa* of *brachah v'hatzlachah* and *gevaltiga siyatah d'shmayah*.

To my *talmid* of yesteryear, present-day colleague, and very best friend, Harav Moshe Greene *shlit"a*: your friendship is invaluable and priceless. You are a true friend in every sense of the word. Your scholarship and clarity of expression, your unusual perceptions and *seichel hayashar*, your uncanny ability to say it as it is, to the *zach*, is *pashut a mechayeh*. The world of *chinuch* and the world of *kiruv* is so much improved because of your magnificent input. Thank you for always being there for me, for sharing with me your astute perceptions, and your encouragement in this project. May you continue to be *mekarev levavos* and *marbitz Torah* in your singular fashion until a hundred and twenty.

I enjoy the *zechus* to be part of a staff of *rebbeim* before whom I am humbled by their erudition, talent, and devotion. To Rabbi Azriel Bodner, Rabbi Yanky Brazil, Rabbi Binyamin Cherney, Rabbi Avraham Davis, Rabbi Avraham Davidowitz, Rabbi Baruch Diamond, Rabbi Michoel Drucksman, Rabbi Yonasan Fischer, Rabbi Shmuel Dovid Halpern, Rabbi Binyamin Jacobi, Rabbi Eliezer Kutner, Rabbi Chaim Majorovic, Rabbi Yaakov Pluchenick, Rabbi Eliyahu Schneider, Rabbi Tzvi Yaakov Stein, Rabbi Yisroel Steinwurtzl, Rabbi Yitzchak Elya

Sussman, and Rabbi Yaakov Tawil, and Rabbi Zissel Zelman, and to colleagues of past years, Rabbi Ahron Rothman, Rabbi Pinny Brooks and Rabbi Mordechai Yehudah Groner; Rabbi Yaakov Oppenheimer, Rabbi Dovid Perlman and Rabbi Ahron Rothman. I thank you for the privilege of your friendship and professionalism as supreme *talmidei chachamim*, and superb *mechanchim* and *marbitzei Torah*.

To my *talmidim*, to whom I owe everything: you have made the *Chazal* of *banecha eilu talmidecha* come alive for me as you have treated me royally as loving children to their father. I only hope that I have responded in kind. You have taught me far more than I have taught you and have given me unending nachas. No doubt, the greatest clarity in understanding comes from giving over to others, and I am indebted to all of those students throughout the years, who afforded me those precious opportunities. The fulfillment that a *rebbi* feels in the growth of his *talmidim* is hard to put into words for it is a *ruchniusdikeh geshmak* that cannot be defined. "אשרי הגבר אשר מלא את אשפתו מהם לא יבשו כי ידברו את אויבים בשער"

I offer a special *Yasher Koach* to the long standing memebers of our twice weekly Gemarah *shiur* of the past twenty years. Together we have completed over a dozen *mesechtos* from which I have gained immeasurably. I am particularly grateful for your *chizuk* and support in this project and the privilege of your friendship. Many thanks to R' Henoch Satt, R' Eliezer Pollack, R' Beryl Elyn, R' Yechiel Rosen, R' Yaakov Klinlowitz, R' Reuvein Dornbush, R' Pinny Solow, R' Dovid Scott, R' Michoel Jacobson, R' Naftali Katz, R' Yissocher Clenman, R' Charley Steinberg, R' Carmi Gruenbaum, R' Levi Miller, and R' Yossi Loeb.

I wish to thank my close talmid R' Yosef Wartelsky for his encouragement and help in the initial stages of this project. I must thank Rabbi Aryeh Mezzi of Judaica Press for not only reviewing this entire manuscript and for the encouragement and professional advice that followed, but for suggesting that I send the manuscript to Israel Book Shop for consideration. At the same time, I am deeply grateful to my dear nephew and niece Rabbi Binyamin and Peninah Sussman who made the initial contact to Rabbi Moshe Kaufman of Israel Book Shop. I am forever grateful to Reb Moshe for his great chizuk in deeming this volume worthy of publication. Reb Moshe, your good name precedes you, and I feel fortunate to have the pleasure of working together with someone who is *malei ne'imus*, and your dedicated staff at Israel Book Shop. A special thank you to Mrs. Liron Delmar of Israel Book Shop for using her professional organizational skills in coordinating this effort. None of this could have progressed without her constant input and advice. In addition, I thank Mr. Sruly Perl for using his expertise in graphic design in creating a cover that enhances and beautifies this work as well as for his artistic flair that has added a significant dimension to this endeavor. I also offer my gratitude to Mr. Ben Schwartz for his great patience and all around contribution in thoroughly giving of himself to see this project through. Many thanks as well to Mrs. Shayndy Abrahamson for her toil in proofreading the manuscript.

A manuscript without an editor is like the icing without the cake or perhaps the cake without the icing. Whichever is the proper metaphor, one thing is for certain; it is far from complete. I am deeply grateful to Mrs. Malkie Gendelman for serving as editor of this volume and for her sensitivity in toiling to preserve my particular style of writing as she persevered in making concrete suggestions and clarifications. It is my hope that in conjunction with your efforts and expertise, the reader will follow the flow of each article for maximum absorption. In addition, I have included a detailed per segment index and outline, to help achieve that objective. A special thanks to Rabbi Moshe Greene and Rabbi Azriel Bodner for their assistance in that effort.

This book could never have come to fruition without the gracious encouragement and enthusiasm of some very dear friends. I offer my heartfelt appreciation to Dr. Baruch and Malkie Eisenberg of Rochester N.Y., Gary and Karen Fragin of Riverdale N.Y., Dr. Baruch and Batya Kassover of Far Rockaway, N.Y., Ed and Rose Leventhal of Harrison, N.Y., Eli and Ronnie Schlossberg of Baltimore, Md, Charley and Naomi Steinberg of Long Beach, N.Y., and Jeffrey and Sharona Weinberg of Woodmere,N.Y. All of you are special Jews with big hearts, whose friendship has enhanced our lives and is valued immeasurably. Thank you for your chizuk.

To our siblings, R' Yaakov and Mindy Sussman, Rabbi Dovid and Dassy Leibtag, Shelly Kurland, Rabbi Dovid and Hindy Sitnick, and Rabbi Zissel and Hadassah Zelman, we feel fortunate to have such brothers and sisters whose closeness and love and devotion we truely cherish. May we merit to join together for many family simchos b'karov.

And now comes the hard part. How does one properly thank his family? To my children, what can I say? Each one of you is precious, each one of you is special baruch Hashem. Our house has always demanded a team effort and you have been the best teammates. Thank you for your participation in our dreams and aspirations. Your contribution has been invaluable. To Yossi and Rivky Freedman of Cleveland, Devorah Esther, Yudi and Chaya Sara Walden Of Monsey, Chanie, Aryeh and Bassy Kurland of Lakewood, Eliyahu Yosef, Chaim Elimelech, Dena, Rissel, Shlomo Meir, and Dovid Shmuel, thank you for being exactly who you are. We are very proud of all of you. May Hashem grant you a shefa of brachah v'hatzlachah in all you endeavor and may we join together very soon b'ezras Hashem, to celebrate many Simchos b'karov

Acharon acharon chaviv; to my partner in life, my wife Leah, I am finally speechless. There are no words. Suffice it to say, you are the captain of the ship, chief navigator and first mate, and much, much more. I can add to the long list your input and encouragement in this endeavor. In your humble and unassuming manner, with a constant smile, and with a tremendous *simchas hachaim*, you are the foundation of all that we have and most certainly my entire support system. *Sheli v'shelahem shelach hu* – With tears of joy in my heart, I thank the *Ribono Shel Olam* for the great gift He has bestowed upon me. May we be *zocheh b'ezras Hashem yisbarach*, to stretch and expand ourselves, together, *l'maan Hashem v'Toraso*, in good health, *Ad me'ah v'esrim shanah, Ad bias go'el tzedek, bimheirah biyameinu, amein.*

"אין אנחנו מספיקים להודות לך ה׳ אלקינו ואלוקי אבותינו ולברך את שמך על אחת מאלף אלפי אלפים ורבי רבבות פעמים הטובות שעשית עם אבותינו ועמנו".

יהושע העשיל שמחה קורלאנד
י״ב מנחם אב תשס״ט
Far Rockaway, N.Y.

Introduction

Communication is a powerful tool that allows mankind to learn from his fellow man and grow and expand. It comes in different forms and shapes and is not restricted to verbal articulation. It can be a facial expression or a physical gesture that may say more than a long essay or lecture. Sometimes it's the passion and the emotion of the speaker, or his tone and decibel. Although, no doubt, the spoken word between those who share a common language and vernacular is most likely to succeed as access to the transmitting of an idea for maximal absorption, nonetheless, at times, people who are lacking in linguistic communication can enjoy a high-level and effective communicatory relationship, as well.

I am reminded of a story that involves the great *gaon* Harav Aharon Kotler *zt"l* and the Mirrer Rosh Yeshivah, Harav Avraham Kalmanowitz *zt"l*. World War II had come to an end when news came to the *Va'ad Hatzalah* (the organization which arranged for the rescue of Jews in Europe from the Holocaust) that twenty-four yeshivah students in Paris were desperately in need of their help. They were in imminent danger of being deported to their country of origin in Eastern Europe, which would have put them at great risk. To the utter surprise of those gathered at the Va'ad Hatzalah meeting, it was suggested by a well-connected activist present that the only person who could help was the notorious head of the Mafia. As it was clearly a matter of *pikuach nefesh*, it was decided that a meeting would be arranged with him, to be attended by Rav Aharon, Rav Avraham, and R' Shlomo Shapiro, the young English speaking head of the organization. The plan was that Rav Aharon would begin speaking in Yiddish in his singular fiery manner, R' Shlomo would translate the Yiddish into English, and Rav Avraham would be there simply to aid in displaying the emotional anguish felt by virtue of these young men's plight. In addition, twenty-thousand dollars in cash was to be brought along to make their case more convincing.

At the meeting, the Mafia boss, dressed in his smoking jacket and puffing a big cigar, snapped at them, "What do you want?"

Rav Aharon began explaining the problem in Yiddish. R' Shlomo, reading the Mafia boss's initial expression of incomprehension, quickly began translating into English, only to be abruptly interrupted by the Mafia boss.

"Hey! You keep quiet and let the Rabbi talk. His words are music to my ears!"

Rav Aharon continued to explain the difficult predicament, as Rav Avraham swayed back and forth, obviously in deep pain. The Mafia boss, having understood the gist of the problem, was clearly affected. Immediately, he asked, "Do you want them to come by boat or by plane?"

"Just as soon as possible," was the unanimous response.

"They will be here Friday!" the Mafia boss responded.

"How much will this cost?" the rabbis asked, expecting to pay the entire twenty-thousand dollars.

"Tell the Rabbi he should give me a blessing instead," was his reply.

Rav Aharon blessed him, and sure enough, two days later, the twenty-four boys arrived safely in New York. Clearly, true communication doesn't involve words as much as the opening of the heart.

One form of communication that all would agree is universal is the language of humor. It is a medium of expression that breaks down barriers. It has an uncanny power to unite two parties, to help absorb and reveal, creating an atmosphere of comfort that eases tension and opens up the heart. A bit of laughter, a smile to one's lips, slowly, but systematically, removes all the partitions that otherwise immobilize and impede the lines of communication.

The Gemara (*Shabbos* 30) explains the *passuk* in *Koheles* (8:15), "And I praised happiness," as Shlomo Hamelech referring to the joy of performing a mitzvah. The Gemara continues by saying that the same is true with regard to teaching Torah. Rashi explains: The *rebbi* should begin his *shiur* with a light matter that will induce laughter.

As an example of the above, the Gemara cites how the great Amora, Rabba, would begin each *shiur* with a *milsa d'bidichusa* – a light matter, stimulating the students' laughter. Rashi explains that the students' hearts were opened by virtue of their joyfulness. The genius of Rabba was to first remove all the barriers and establish a rapport, so that the words of Torah that flowed from his heart would enter theirs.

Simchah – joyfulness – has the amazing power to inspire expansion. The likeness of the word *simchah* and *tzemichah* (growth) indicates as much. The Gemara tells us that the *Shechinah* only rests in an atmosphere of *simchah shel mitzvah* – the joyfulness brought about by *mitzvos*. Elisha the prophet, when, at the behest of King Yehoshafat, was asked to inquire the word of Hashem in regard to their war plans, instructs, "'*But now bring me a minstrel.' And it was, when the minstrel played, that the Hand of Hashem came upon him (Melachim II 3:15).*" For the Spirit of the Divine Presence to rest upon him, Elisha first needed to expand in order to accommodate it. The joyous response to the sounds of the musicians allowed for that expansion.

One of the many ongoing miracles in the Beis Hamikdash was that no matter how crowded it was, there was always plenty of room for everyone when they prostrated themselves before Hashem. This was not simply an isolated miracle, but rather, it underscores the very essence of the Beis Hamikdash as a symbol of man's ability to stretch himself and transcend all earthly limitations. When one humbles himself before Hashem, he builds himself into an abode for the *Shechinah*, having expanded himself to be that vessel that can house the Divine Presence. The Beis Hamikdash is the symbolic representation that a concentration of something as holy as the *Shechinah* can exist in this world. But the goal is not the physical edifice in and of itself; it is the inspiration thereof to make oneself into a miniature Beis Hamikdash, expanding his *kochos haneshamah* to their fullest. However, the *Shechinah* can only rest where there is *simchah*, for it is *simchah* that opens the heart and allows one to develop into a receptacle for it.

Chazal's choice of terminology to express the difference in measure between a handbreadth of a tightly clasped fist and a more relaxed grip, is *tefach atzeiv* as opposed to *tefach socheik*. *Tefach atzeiv*, the constricted measure, literally means "a somber handbreadth," while the more expansive one, *tefach socheik*, literally means "a happy handbreadth." *Chazal*, in their great wisdom, are incidentally teaching us a lesson for life: When one is happy, he is expansive, his horizons broadened, his range extended. He is ripened for absorption; he is a sponge ready to soak everything in. He has enjoyed a time to laugh; now it's time to listen!

Between Man and G-d

Fear of Heaven – Yours for the Asking

Bernie was a good and pious man. When he passed away, G-d Himself greeted Bernie in Heaven, and asked if he would like something to eat.

"I could eat something," replied Bernie. So G-d opened up a can of tuna and they shared it.

While eating his humble meal, Bernie looked down into the underworld. He noticed that the inhabitants there were devouring steak, pheasant, pastries, and quality Scotch; Johnny Walker Blue Label, no less.

The next day, G-d approached Bernie again and asked if he was hungry. Bernie, again, answered in the affirmative.

Once again, a can of tuna was opened and shared, while down below, Bernie couldn't help but notice a feast of caviar, champagne, lamb chops, truffle, brandy, and chocolates.

The next day, mealtime arrived, and another can of tuna was opened.

Meekly, Bernie approached G-d and said, "I don't get it! My whole life I labored to develop fear of Heaven, so that one day I would merit a place in Heaven. Now I'm here, and all I get to eat is tuna! But in that other place, they eat like kings! I just don't understand!"

"To be honest," G-d replied, "for just the two of us, it doesn't pay to cook!"

Perhaps the most difficult achievement in *avodas* Hashem, serving G-d, is to develop *yiras Shamayim*, fear of Heaven. In a world that champions independence and the free spirit, we fear nothing, let alone the abstract. *Time* magazine took care of G-d a long time ago, when they so audaciously displayed the headline on their cover, "Is G-d Dead?"

Even Torah-observant Jews have difficulty attaining true *yiras Shamayim*. The Gemara in *Brachos* (33b) questions Moshe Rabbeinu's reference to fear of Heaven as but a small matter. The *passuk* (*Devarim* 10:12) says, "And now, Yisrael, what is it that Hashem your G-d asks from you? Simply to fear Hashem..."

The Gemara asks: "*Simply* to fear Him? Is fear of Heaven a small matter?" Why, it is *Hakadosh Baruch Hu's* greatest treasure; His greatest prize! The Gemara answers that indeed, for Moshe Rabbeinu, it was a small matter.

The question, however, still remains: Moshe Rabbeinu, the great leader of Klal Yisrael, was handpicked to lead them. He was chosen when he was a shepherd, because he was sensitive to the individual needs of each one of his sheep. Undoubtedly, Moshe Rabbeinu possessed the insight to understand and to relate to the common Jew, and comprehend his struggles and challenges, even in the area of *yiras Shamayim*. Nonetheless, Moshe still refers to *yiras Shamayim* as but a small thing. Moshe was clearly sending us a message that fear of Heaven is not only available and accessible to great people like himself; rather, it is attainable for everyone. And yet, the description of *yiras Shamayim* as a simple matter is still troubling. How can it be a simple matter?

The Kotzker *zt"l* enlightens us with his explanation of a well-known *Chazal* (*Brachos* 33b): "*Hakol b'yedei Shamayim chutz mi'yiras Shamayim* – Everything is in the Hands of Heaven, except for fear of Heaven." The Kotzker interprets this to apply to the realm of prayer. Everything we beseech from Hashem in prayer may or may not be granted. Acquiescence to such requests is solely in the *Ribono Shel Olam's* hands. Not so when we pray for *yiras Shamayim*. If we sincerely ask for it, if we want it badly enough, we are guaranteed that our wish will be granted. Every prayer is in the hands of Heaven except for our prayers for fear of Heaven. *That* is in our hands, guaranteed for the asking.

When we *bentch* Rosh Chodesh on Shabbos Mevarchim, there appears to be a redundancy in our request for *yiras Shamayim*. We entreat Hashem for "*yiras Shamayim v'yiras cheit* – fear of Heaven and fear of sin." And once again, in the last line, we ask for "*ahavas Torah v'yiras Shamayim* –

love of Torah, and fear of Heaven." In truth, though, it is not a redundancy at all. At first when we pray for fear of Heaven, we're praying for its two essential levels; *yiras ha'onesh* – fear of punishment; and the loftier *yiras haromimus* – awe of His exaltedness. Subsequently, we *daven* that we should develop a *love* for *yiras Shamayim*, similar to the love for Torah that we desire (as though the *tefillah* read *ahavas Torah "v'ahavas" yiras Shamayim*). For if we will love and appreciate *yiras Shamayim*, we will pray for it; and if we pray for it, our prayers will be answered.

Moshe Rabbeinu taught us that fear of Heaven, unique among all that we crave, is in fact a simple thing for every Jew to obtain. He understood that through sincere prayer, it is accessible to all. Our problem arises when we don't really crave it. We are terrified that it might cramp our style and interfere with many objects in life that have become our obsessions and toys. If only we wanted it, we could have it, and add precious jewels to the *Ribono Shel Olam's* cherished treasure chest in Heaven. The *passuk* itself hints to the above explanation. It says "... *Mah Hashem Elokecha sho'eil me'imach ki im l'yirah...*" The words "*sho'eil me'imach* – ask from [within] you," lead to "*ki im l'yirah* – simply to fear G-d." If one asks from within himself with sincere yearning to acquire *yiras Shamayim*, it will be, as Moshe Rabbeinu described it, a simple matter to fear Hashem, for it can become his for the asking.

Has Anyone Seen My Father?

A man approached the ringmaster of the circus, hoping to join the circus as a lion-tamer.

"Do you have any experience?" the ringmaster asked.

"Experience? Why, of course! My father, of blessed memory, was a world-famous lion-tamer!" the man exclaimed. "He taught me everything he knew."

"Really?" said the ringmaster. "Did he teach you how to make a lion jump through a flaming hoop?"

"Oh, absolutely," the man responded.

"Have you ever had eight lions form a pyramid?" the ringmaster continued.

"Oh, that's one of my favorites!" the man answered enthusiastically.

Quite impressed, the circus leader pressed on. "Have you ever stuck your head in a lion's mouth?"

Here the man had a different response. "Just once," he answered.

"Why only once?" the ringmaster inquired.

The man answered, "I was looking for my father!"

Chazal tell us that "*Yaakov Avinu lo meis* – our father Yaakov never died." Many understand this to mean that the legacy of Yaakov Avinu lives on in every Jew. Within each Yid, there exists the potential to actualize an inbred *koach* that was put in his *neshamah* from Yisrael Saba. It is imperative that we understand the essence of our forefather Yaakov, so that we can come in contact with this congenital capacity.

The Torah portrays Yaakov Avinu as an "*ish tam yoshev ohalim* – a wholesome man who resided in the tents of Torah study." Targum Yonosan Ben Uziel translates this phrase as "one who strove for greatness before Hashem." This same expression of "one who strove for greatness" is used by Targum Onkelos to define the term "*mevakeish* Hashem" in *Parshas Ki Sisa*. (There, we find Moshe Rabbeinu removing his tent far from the camp, so that all who sought Hashem ("*kol mevakeish Hashem*") would have to venture outside of their familiar surroundings.)

Clearly, the essence of Yaakov Avinu, in a word, was that he was a *mevakeish* Hashem, He sought any possible means to develop his relationship with his Creator, his yearning for spiritual greatness insatiable. He used every medium at his disposal to enhance this relationship with his Father in Heaven. He understood that Torah study was of prime importance to enable him to achieve this goal, and to this end spent fourteen years of sleepless nights in the *beis medrash* of Shem v'Eiver. He had but one mission in life: to find his Father, the *Eibishter*, to know Him and to draw close to Him. He was the quintessential *mevakeish* Hashem.

The story is told of a wealthy man who was seeking a *shidduch* for his daughter. An eminent *talmid chacham* in his own right, the wealthy man approached a *rosh yeshivah* with a proposition in hand. He asked that he be allowed to ask a Talmudic question to the students in the *beis medrash*, with the intent to reward the young man who could answer his question, with his daughter's hand in marriage. The stage was set, and the question was presented. The ensuing debates among the young men in the yeshivah were heated, and the sound of Torah echoed far beyond the walls of the *beis medrash*. Nevertheless, when the time came for the wealthy man to leave, nobody had come up with a satisfactory answer for the question. The rich man boarded his coach and began to leave the confines of the yeshivah, when a young man, running as fast as he could, called out to him, "Please, stop! Don't go yet!"

"What is it?" asked the wealthy man. "Have you an answer to my question?"

"No," responded the young man, "I have no answer to your question, but please don't leave before you tell us the answer!"

The wealthy man smiled. "This is precisely the type of young man I was seeking," he said. "I wasn't seeking someone who could answer my question, as much as someone who is a *mevakeish*, who, like you, wants to know the answer. I would be privileged to have you as my son-in-law."

Harav Chaim Shmulevitz *zt"l* was once visiting his uncle, the Novaradok Rosh Yeshivah, Harav Avraham Yoffin *zt"l*, in Bialystok. As they toured the *beis medrash*, Rav Chaim asked his uncle to show him the outstanding students in the yeshivah. Rav Avraham gestured toward various young men, as he pointed out the biggest *lamdan*, the biggest *masmid*, the biggest *amkan*, and the biggest *baki*.

Finally, Rav Chaim asked him, "Tell me, who is the best *bachur* in the yeshivah?"

Rav Avraham took his nephew to a corner of the *beis medrash* and pointed to a young man. "He's the best *bachur* in the yeshivah!"

Rav Chaim, a bit perplexed, asked his uncle, "How could this *bachur* be the best in the yeshivah, when he's not the biggest *lamdan*, *amkan*, *masmid*, or *baki*? What exactly makes him the best boy in the yeshivah?"

Rav Avraham replied, "He is the biggest *mevakeish* in the yeshivah!" Indeed, this young man grew up to become one of the most outstanding *talmidei chachamim* of his generation, the great Steipler Gaon *zt"l*.

Years ago, various religious groups popularized bumper stickers as a means to advertise their tainted message. Some read, "I've found it!" while others read, "I never even lost it!" Soon to follow was, "I ain't even looking for it!" Unfortunately, this has become the creed of society at large, and too many of our brothers and sisters in kind. They are not seeking the magnificent legacy of Yaakov Avinu that is theirs. They are not in tune with their forefather Yaakov, who could help connect them to their Father in Heaven. They "ain't even looking for it!"

But *baruch* Hashem, there are many who are searching. The remnant of Yisrael Saba stirs within. The spirit of the *mevakeish* bustles about. For many, it's a long road that takes them around the world. For others, it is a series of *Shabbatonim* and retreats, trips to Israel, or a visit to the Western Wall. Our task as those fortunate enough be among the *mevakshei* Hashem is, first and foremost, to actualize our *kochos* in this endeavor, and, in turn, inspire others to connect to the bequest of Yaakov Avinu, and ultimately connect them with their Father in Heaven. We look forward to the day when all of Klal Yisrael will find happiness in the spirit of the *passuk*, "*Yismach lev mevakshei Hashem* – The hearts of those who seek Hashem will rejoice." (*Divrei Hayamim I* 16:9)

I Don't Even Know You

A man was approached by a mugger in Brooklyn and had no cash in his pocket. Petrified that he might be physically attacked by his assailant, he took out his checkbook and nervously said, "L-l-let me write you out a check!"

"A check? I should take a check from you? I should trust you with a check?" the mugger screamed at him. "Why, I don't even know you!"

―――

In the unraveling of society, its morals and standards, people have lost the mutual trust that once was a given. With the 2008 fall of the economy and the bankruptcy of so many "worthy" institutions in which people had placed their trust, not to mention their life savings, consumer confidence has sunken to an all-time low. Personal greed and money-hoarding has become public knowledge, leaving behind a trail of unfortunate victims. Politicians have used their positions to benefit themselves at the expense of their own constituency. Credit markets are hesitant to lend and investors are reluctant to endow, creating a flip-flop, topsy-turvy, here-today-gone-tomorrow, unpredictable global meltdown that has the whole world shaking. It all boils down to one thing: a world-wide lack of trust.

As our current exile has evolved, we have endured many a disappointment in the decadent behavior of mankind, losing faith in the human experience in the process. And although we would, nonetheless, like to believe that there still exists some semblance of decency and integrity in this world, as time goes on, one thing or another diminishes that dream. The events of the fall of 2008 have wreaked havoc on our reliance on our fellow man, and have weakened man's resolve to work harmoniously in the spirit of *"zeh neheneh v'zeh lo chaseir* – everybody gains and nobody loses."

Dovid Hamelech warned us many times about placing too much faith in mankind. "Do not place your trust in nobles, nor in human beings." (*Tehillim* 146:3) "Praiseworthy is he whose help is the G-d of Yaakov, whose hope is in Hashem, his G-d." (*Tehillim* 146:5) No doubt, our misappropriated faith in man is commensurate with our inadequate faith in the *Ribono Shel Olam*. *Parnassah* – sustenance – has the same numerical value of *neshamah* – soul. *Parnassah* lies in the realm of the spiritual. Our fiscal success is inextricably linked to the Source of all sustenance. It is the domain of the One Who "opens His

Hands and satisfies the desires of every living thing" (*Tehillim* 145:16). As the *passuk* says, "*He who places his trust in Hashem, will be surrounded by (His) kindness.*" (*Tehillim* 32:10) When we show the *Ribono Shel Olam* that it is in Him that we trust, that it is not "*my power and the strength of my hand that has produced for me all these riches,*" (Devarim 8:17) but rather that it is the Hand of Hashem that determines a person's sustenance, then indeed we will be showered with His blessing.

The Gemara in *Taanis* (8) brings the following: Rav Ami said, "Come and see how great are the people who have faith in G-d!" He explains that we learn this from the story of the weasel and the pit. Rashi elaborates: There was a girl who fell into a pit. A boy came by and promised to rescue her on the condition that she would marry him one day. The girl consented, and they made the pit and a passing weasel witnesses to their agreement. They went their separate ways until they grew older. When the girl became of marriageable age, she kept her word and didn't marry anyone else, waiting for this boy. The boy, though, married another woman, who bore him two sons. Calamity befell both children. The first was killed by a weasel, and the second fell into a pit and died. The young man's wife asked him why such tragedy had befallen them, and he relayed the story of his broken promise. Upon his wife's suggestion, he divorced her and married the girl he had saved, as he had originally promised.

The Gemara deduces a monumental lesson from this incident through a *kal v'chomer*: If one who trusts in a weasel and a pit has his trust honored to such an extent, one who trusts in *Hakadosh Baruch Hu*, all the more so, is his trust honored. The primary effort one needs to put forth in order to be sustained is acquiring the *middah* of *bitachon* in *Hakadosh Baruch Hu*, believing that He will provide him with *parnassah*. Surely a weasel and a pit have no power to bring about someone's death, but, notwithstanding this, the power of *emunah* is so great, that the young couple's trust in them empowered them. How much more so will our steadfast belief in Hashem as the Source of all life, "empower," as if it were, and inspire an outpouring of blessing and an overflow of sustenance. Such is the power of *bitachon*.

It is not at all surprising that the Gemara there mentions, as well, that rain descends from Heaven only in the merit of the people of faith, for it is precisely these people who inspire the overflow from Heaven, in the realm of "*tnu oz l'Elokim* – give strength to Hashem" (*Tehillim* 68:35). By showing our full trust in Hashem, we "allow" Him, as if it were, to be forthcoming with all His goodness, which is His greatest wish.

The Kli Yakar writes in explaining the severity of the prohibition of *ribbis* (usury), that it removes a person from the *middah* of *bitachon*. The person becomes reliant on the guaranteed perk of the interest income, and his eyes are not raised toward Heaven as they should be. The "get rich quick" philosophy of American society has its affect on our level of *bitachon*. Rolling the die in a casino gamble and playing the numbers on Wall Street are not vastly different. Although it is commendable to work diligently to provide for one's family, frivolous gambles encroach on one's *bitachon* in Hashem through their power of fantasy and illusion. *Baalei bitachon* are realists of the highest accord. Their *bitachon* is a trust built upon the truth about Hashem, that everything is in the Hands of Heaven, with few exceptions (*yiras Shamayim* and *tzinim pachim*), and that the more one makes that trust the foundation of his life, the more overflow of blessing will stream forth from Hashem's vast storehouse. The *middah* of *bitachon* is not merely a praiseworthy approach to one's service of Hashem; it is the catalyst for all the blessings of life, for all the *yeshuos* we so sorely need. It is the boost of positive energy that serves as the impetus for all of Hashem's graciousness and kindness.

The Navi laments, "*The ox knows its master, the donkey the trough that feeds him, [but] my people don't know [their Master – Hashem].*" (*Yeshayah* 1:3) We must make it known to our Creator that we know Him, that we trust in Him, and that we grant Him credit, as He is the sole Source of our existence.

It Ain't Just Luck

Steve leaves his Upper West Side brownstone at 777 West 77th Street at exactly 7:00 A.M. to catch the 7:07 Seventh Avenue Express. On the way to the train, he notices a manila envelope with no name or address on the ground before him, at the corner of 7th Avenue and 77th Street. Curious as to its contents, he quickly picks it up and finds it filled with $100 bills. Frantically, he counts them, amazed at his good fortune to have found $7,700.

"Today must be my lucky day!" he exclaims in delight, seven being a lucky number.

Steve stuffs the cash into his pockets, and having missed his train, hails a cab instead, to complete his commute to his office at 77 7th Avenue. His excitement is further intrigued, when the cab driver pulls up in front of his building and tells him the fare is exactly seven dollars and seventy seven cents.

"Today must be my lucky day!" he shouts out again. "I'm not going to work! I'm going to the racetrack! Driver, take me to Belmont Park Racetrack in Long Island!"

Steve is further encouraged when, upon arriving at Belmont, the taxi fare comes to exactly seventy seven dollars and seventy seven cents. "There's no doubt about it! Today is my lucky day!" he rejoices, as he rushes in to place his bet. There it is on the charts. Seventh Heaven is running at the odds of seven to one in the seventh race.

"$7,777 on Seventh Heaven in the seventh race," he orders the teller, positive that today is his lucky day, and seven is his lucky number.

Sure enough, she came in seventh!

In the superficial existence of a secular world devoid of depth and meaning, good-luck charms and rabbit's feet are popularly cherished. The notion of something a little more esoteric would be one's Zodiac sign, as a source for predicting character or innate tendencies. "Hi, I'm a Leo!" "Hi, I'm a Gemini!" Presto! A match made in Heaven! Chinese fortune cookies have even invaded the kosher market as a favorite part of the menu of that cuisine. Las Vegas and Atlantic City have gained enormously from such shallowness, which unfortunately has made a major contribution to gambling addictions and the like. Such behavior runs the gamut from the stock market to every conceivable sporting event, from the sophisticated to the contemptible. To our dismay, this has also penetrated the Orthodox Jewish community.

Chazal, however, to whom we turn to for all of our guidance in life, tell us unequivocally *(Shabbos 156a)* "Ein mazel *l'Yisrael"*. The relationship between Klal Yisrael and the world is not governed by constellations, i.e. the revolving forces that are associated with the course of events. Although *mazel* is certainly part of the Divine Plan and governs a specific domain for Klal Yisrael (e.g. we wish one another *mazel tov* at all joyous occasions), it is by no means the end-all. We are privileged to enjoy a special relationship with our Creator that precludes such limitation and extends beyond the world of *mazel*. Indeed, idol-worshippers are referred to using the acronym of *"aku"m,"* namely, *ovdei kochavim u'mazalos* – people who worship the stars and the constellations, without any specific mention of molten images or statues that typify idolatry. For a Jew to place his hopes and dreams or his fortune in "good luck" is a distortion of the role he plays in Hashem's world. It is at times the beginning of the denial of the truth that can lead to even such frivolity as idolatry. One of the reasons a gambler is precluded from being a witness in a Jewish court (*Mishnah Sanhedrin* 3:3) is because he is not involved in *"yishuvo shel olam,"* the settling of the world. Not only does he not pursue gainful employment in the practical sense, he grossly misunderstands his unique and important mission, that of bettering his world and destiny. He is preoccupied with the foolishness of chance, when his investments should be in the futures of this world and the next. We dare not gamble away our eternal reward for a thrill or two. Our stocks and securities are our good deeds and their merit, and they are not on the table for any wager whatsoever.

The Gemara (*Shabbos* 32a) discusses auspicious moments in life, when a person might be more susceptible to Heavenly judgment and punishment. The Gemara cites the story of Rav Yanai, who would never cross a bridge without first checking its security. He said, "A person should never treat any situation of chance or potential danger lightly, for who knows if he will be worthy of a miracle that will save him? And even if he is, he will lose precious *zechuyos* (merits) in the process."

The creed of great *tzaddikim (Bereishis 32:1)* is always: "*katonti mikol hachassadim* – perhaps I am unworthy or have already exhausted all of my merits." They are fully aware of the ongoing grace of Hashem, and the precarious balance of our *zechuyos*. To chance the loss of even one *zechus* for any venture, let alone capricious behavior, is out of the question.

And yet, even within the confines of observant Jewry, too many are caught up in their world of adventure and risk. From bungee-jumping to snow-boarding; from jet-skiing to parasailing and sky-diving, from binge-eating to alcohol consumption, people cross all types of bridges, banking on their frivolous "E-ZPass" philosophy of living for the moment and reveling in good luck charms.

Our good fortune lies in one number: the number one. The Oneness of Hashem and our relationship with Him, determines the foundational strength of the bridges we cross in life. As the Kotzker *zt"l* explained about "*Echad Mi Yode'a*," the song in the *Haggadah*, everything in creation connects to the *mitzvos* of the Torah, since the Torah is the blueprint of creation *(Zohar Hakadosh, Terumah 161)*. Who knows why the word "one" exists in the world? For one singular reason: to recognize Hashem as the Source of it all; for all to proclaim "*Echad Elokainu bashamayim u'vaaretz;*" for all to decree in unison, "*Shema Yisrael ...Hashem Echad* – Hear O Israel ... Hashem is One."

Sing His Praises O You Nations

Two elderly women were out for a Sunday drive in the old Lincoln Continental. Both could barely see over the dashboard. Cruising along, they came to an intersection. The light was red, but they went right through.

Sadie, in the passenger seat, thought to herself, "I must be losing it. I could have sworn we just went through a red light."

After a few more minutes, they came to another intersection where the light was red, and again they zipped right through it. This time, Sadie really was concerned that maybe her age had finally caught up with her, and she decided to pay very close attention at the next light.

Sure enough, at the next intersection, the light was definitely red, and they went right through.

Sadie, now sure of herself, turned to her friend and said, "Mildred! Did you know we just ran three lights in a row? You could have killed us!"

Mildred turned to her and said, "Oh! Am I driving?"

At times we live in absolute oblivion. We easily get lost in our own thoughts, spaced out and in total "la la land". Even when completely alert, we would be foolish and naive to think we know all that transpires around us. We forget so quickly that we are mere mortals with limited vision and foresight. How many times have we been driving and changed lanes while lost in thought, unmindful to the rapidly approaching vehicle in the next lane, and escaping calamity by a fraction of a second? *"They encircle me, they also surround me; in the Name of Hashem I cut them down."* (*Tehillim* 118:10) Dovid Hamelech teaches us to realize that we are surrounded! Unbeknown to us, things are happening around us all the time, events which threaten our very existence, and only Hashem saves us each time.

It is difficult to read the news about all of the animosity that exists in the world toward our Jewish brethren. We find the threats of annihilation even in a post-Nazi world of supposed tolerance, the dimensions of anti-Semitism in a "politically correct" society repugnant and shocking. We become so absorbed in our sighing, "When will the *yeshuah* (salvation) come?" that we lose sight of all the many *yeshuos* that *do* occur on an ongoing basis.

Dovid Hamelech expressed this thought in a chapter in *Tehillim* so beautifully that it was incorporated in the *Hallel*: *"Praise Hashem all nations, exalt Him all people, for His kindness is overwhelming to us (the Jewish People), and the truth of Hashem is eternal, Hallelukah."* (117:1-2)

The question is raised: If there is any one reason why the non-Jews hate us, it is because of the preferential treatment Klal Yisrael enjoys as a "favored nation," and the privileged relationship we have with our Father in Heaven. One wouldn't think in his wildest dreams that the reason for the nations of the world to praise Hashem would be the overwhelming kindness and favor He shows Klal Yisrael. If anything, the exact opposite should be true! Yet the *passuk* states that precisely because of Hashem's magnanimity to us – the non-Jewish nations' sworn enemy – they should praise Hashem! This begs for explanation.

In truth, Dovid Hamelech alluded to the explanation we seek in a different chapter of *Tehillim*. He wrote: *"Why do the peoples gather, and the nations talk in vain? The kings of the earth take their stand, and the princes conspire secretly against Hashem and His anointed one. 'Let us cut off their cords. Let us cast off their ropes from ourselves.' He who sits in Heaven will laugh; Hashem will mock them."* (2:1-4)

We are ignorant of the myriad times the nations of the world have plotted to destroy us, only to have their plans foiled by the One Above. We are unaware of the miracles and wonders that the *Ribono Shel Olam* does on our behalf, saving us time and again from their ugly intent. Even the supernatural protection from thirty-nine scud missiles during the Gulf War, all launched directly at our people, failed to awaken us to this ongoing phenomenon.

But *they* know! The nations of the world, be they the despots and anarchists of tyrannical reign, the "aristocrats" of the

European Union, or the "sophisticates" of the United Nations, all know of their intent to destroy, slander, undermine, and connive, and they know how Hashem constantly disturbs their grandiose plans. Ironically, it is only they, who are fully cognizant of all their evil plots and how time after time Hashem has intervened, who can stand up and proclaim His praises. Yes, indeed, because Hashem has shown overwhelming kindness to Klal Yisrael, the nations of the world shall exalt His holy Name, and most certainly shall we, the privileged recipients of His ongoing redemption.

Between Man and Himself

Oblivious

Marty and his wife, Sadie, hadn't spoken in days. Each was stubborn, neither wanting to give in. But now, Marty had a dilemma: Tomorrow would be the big fishing trip with Phil, and he needed to be woken up early for it. Heavy sleeper that he was, he wanted to ask his wife to wake him up at 5:00 a.m. so he'd make it for his 5:30 departure, but he didn't want to be the first to break the silence. How could he get her to do him this favor without giving in? He decided to leave a note asking her to please wake him up at 5:00 a.m.

The next morning, Marty overslept and didn't wake up until 9:30. Realizing that he'd missed his ride, he frantically looked for his wife, furious at her for not waking him. All he found was a note: "Good morning! It's 5:00 a.m."

Chazal tell us that one is blind to his own shortcomings. He may easily see them in others, yet is often foolishly ignorant of his own inadequacies. Like a *nega*, a plague, his *negius* (subjectivity) is a malady that has a cataract affect, impairing the vision of even the most astute and wise.

Rav Dessler *zt"l* discusses the subtle and subconscious *negius* of Eliezer, the servant of Avraham Avinu, upon his appointment as his master's agent to find a wife for Yitzchak. He contrasts the original conversation between Eliezer and Avraham, and Eliezer's subsequent repetition of that conversation in the house of Besuel and Lavan.

Initially, Eliezer asks Avraham: *"Perhaps the woman will not wish to come with me. Shall I bring Yitzchak to her?"* (*Bereishis* 24:5) It should be noted that "*ulai* – perhaps" is spelled *malei* (in its complete form, i.e. with a *vav*). Subsequently, after seeing the Divine message indicating that Rivka is the Heavenly ordained wife for Yitzchak, Eliezer repeats his original conversation with Avraham to Lavan and Besuel. He says: *"And I said to my master, 'Perhaps the woman will refuse to come with me.'"* (ibid. 24:39) Although Eliezer repeats the very same dilemma, this time the word "*ulai* – perhaps" is spelled *chasser* (in its shorter version, i.e. without a *vav*), which can also be read as "*eilai*," meaning "to me." Rashi comments, at the point of this second conversation, that Eliezer had his own daughter, and he was secretly hoping that Avraham would select her to be Yitzchak's wife. The *passuk's* usage of the abridged spelling of the word "*ulai* – perhaps," which can also be read as "*eilai* – to me," hints at this idea.

It is peculiar that the Torah alludes to Eliezer's secret self-interest at this point, and not during the initial conversation. After all, it is more likely that Eliezer's inner desire surfaced initially, rather than in this later conversation, which took place after he had already been shown by Heaven that it was Rivka who was Divinely ordained for Yitzchak. Would it not have been preferable to spell "*ulai* – perhaps" in its abridged form in the initial conversation?

Rav Dessler explains: *Negius* is so overwhelming, that it precludes the possibility of any awareness or cognizance of its presence. As long as the possibility that Eliezer's mission might fail still existed, leaving open the option of having his daughter marry Yitzchak, he was blinded to any personal subjectivity. Such is the essence of someone who is *noge'a b'davar* – biased about something. It was only later, after Eliezer knew unequivocally that Rivka was clearly Yitzchak's *basherte*, and the option of having his daughter marry Yitzchak was ruled out, that he was able to recognize the truth, that he had been a *noge'a b'davar*. The Torah, therefore, purposely hints to this specifically in the later conversation; for it was only then, when all *negius* had dissipated, that his prior subjectivity was revealed.

Such is the power of subjectivity. As the *passuk* (*Devarim* 16:19) testifies, "*For a bribe will blind the eyes of the wise and make the words of the righteous crooked.*" One could well imagine that if even great *talmidei chachamim* and *tzaddikim* are subject to such oblivion when *negius* prevails, how much more so are we.

Priorities

Bernie was shocked to see an empty seat in the row ahead of him at the Super Bowl. Feeling somewhat bold, he asked the woman seated next to the empty seat, "Excuse me, but whose seat is that?"

"Oh! That's my husband's seat," the woman replied.

"Well, where is he?" Bernie inquired, perhaps overstepping his bounds. "He'll miss the kickoff!"

The lady answered, "Oh, he passed away!"

"I'm terribly sorry," Bernie lamented, silently scolding himself for allowing his curiosity to get the better of him and acting so nosy. But never one to control his mouth, he persisted. "Excuse me for asking one more question. Didn't any of your relatives want the seat?"

"Oh, no!" the lady answered. "They all insisted on going to the funeral!"

Misplaced priorities, you might say, at its worst. Yet at times, we are not far behind in our distorted hierarchy of precedence and preference. Growing up in America, we develop many loves and interests, all of which quickly become part of our very being. Parting from them or even relegating them to a lower position on the chart becomes quite difficult, if not impossible. It is inconceivable to establish a true measure of one's priorities when everything is important. On top of that, we live in an environment in which people are accustomed to getting everything and wanting it all, which invariably leads to a situation where the truly crucial areas of life are unfairly shared with the less significant ones.

The Chiddushei Harim said it best: The Gemara in *Sanhedrin*, in the course of discussing the issue of *yehareg v'al ya'avor* (when one must relinquish his very life rather than transgress a prohibition), cites the *passuk* of "*V'ahavta eis Hashem Elokecha b'chol levavecha uv'chol nafshecha uv'chol me'odecha* – You should love Hashem your G-d with all of your heart, with all of your soul, and with all of your resources." (*Devarim* 6:5) The Gemara proceeds to *darshan* - infer: "*B'chol nafshecha* - With all of your soul; *Afilu noteil es nafshecha* – even if that love of Hashem, at times, demands that one relinquish his soul." This *drasha* serves as the source for one's obligation to surrender his life rather than serve idolatry (the antithesis of love of Hashem).

The Chiddushei Harim suggests homiletically that perhaps a similar *drasha* could be made regarding the accompanying words: "*B'chol levavecha* - With all of your heart; *Afilu noteil es levavecha* – love Hashem with all of your heart, even if it means one must give up his heart," (and all its many loves) for the sake of *ahavas* Hashem.

Yes, indeed! One must even give up the Super Bowl for the sake of a higher priority, such as his afternoon *seder*. He may have to give up Dunkin' Donuts for the sake of *chalav* Yisrael. He will have to put to pasture his previously cherished choice of entertainment and relaxation because it doesn't meet with proper Torah standards. Whereas the previous generation, much to our sadness, was subjected to *nisyonos* (challenges) in the realm of "*b'chol nafshecha* – with all of your soul," challenges of actual *mesiras nefesh* where many courageously gave up their lives *al kiddush* Hashem, the primary *nisayon* of our generation might very well be of the "*b'chol levavecha* – with all of your heart" variety. In our generation, the primary challenge facing us is that of giving up our hearts and relinquishing our grasp on the numerous playthings of our American youth, in order to prioritize our lives, once and for all, in a focused and orderly fashion.

"*Lulei Torascha sha'ashu'ai* – were it not for Your Torah, my preoccupation" – were it not for Your Torah, my preoccupation, my priority, my comfort, my plaything, my most cherished commodity, "*az avadti b'anyi* – then I would have perished in my affliction" (*Tehillim* 119:92) – then I would have perished in the affliction and pain, and the ensuing confusion, of not knowing where to place the emphasis. Dovid Hamelech knew so well what is to be cherished and what is to be discarded, and how crucial it is to make those choices, so as not to sink in the quicksand of mediocrity.

May we merit to have the clarity of vision to understand where to place the proper emphasis, as we filter through the vicissitudes of life, and may we focus our attention on His will as the primary ideal and fundamental principle of our existence.

What's in a Name?

The charming and dashing presidential candidate confidently entered the nursing home with his entourage, and approached an elderly lady in a wheelchair.

"Good morning, ma'am! How are you today?

The old lady didn't give him the time of day.

"Ma'am, do you know who I am? Do you know my name?"

Again, the old lady all but ignored him.

Speaking a little louder this time, he said, "Ma'am, are you sure you don't recognize me? Do you know my name?"

"No, I don't know your name," she replied, "but if you go to the front desk, I'm sure they can help you find it!"

The Gemara (*Yoma* 83) tells us regarding Rabbi Meir: "*dayeik bishma*" - he exhibited caution with respect to a person's name, and thereby avoided lodging in a certain inn whose proprietor's name connoted dishonesty. In fact, the *sefarim* tell us that parents, when naming a child, are inspired with a spirit of *ruach hakodesh* of sorts, and the chosen name reflects the essence of that child and his potential. At the *bris*, all proclaim, "Just as he entered the *bris*, so should he enter to Torah, *chuppah*, and good deeds." The very name he is given at the *bris* will directly reflect upon his ultimate accomplishments in life's most crucial areas of Torah, marriage and family, and good deeds.

The mishnah (*Makkos* 4) discusses whether it is proper to administer two punishments (monetary payment and thirty-nine lashes) for one violation. In contrast to the opinion of the rabbis that the *passuk* dictates that one not receive two punishments, *kol ham'shaleim eino lokeh*, Rabbi Meir insists that when the source of each punishment is a separate *passuk*, both penalties are to be administered. He states: "*Shelo hasheim* - For the Scriptural verse that is the source for the punishment of lashes is not the same as the one that is the source for monetary payment." It is interesting to note that he uses the word "*sheim* – name" to mean "source or origin". One's name, and the reputation that he builds during the course of his lifetime, are inseparably linked to his origin, to the root of his *neshamah*, to his uniqueness and individual portion in Torah as one of the 600,000 *neshamos* of Klal Yisrael. His name is a mere hint to his purpose in life, as he strives to equate his earthly performance with its parallel Heavenly expectation. Indeed, the numerical value of the word "*sheim*– name," which is 340, is equal to the numerical value of the word "*mekor* – source". A name is not a simple matter.

How unfortunate it is that so many, merely for the sake of blending in with their Western culture environs, have abandoned their Hebrew names in favor of these names' English counterparts. The "*Yiddishe nummen*" (Jewish name) is reserved for, and invoked at, special occasions only, like the *bris*, bar mitzvah, and eulogy. The Seths and the Scotts, the Jessicas and the Jennifers abound all around us. Even more unfortunate is the loss of perspective of one's purpose in life and personal mandate from Hashem. There is a source to his existence, the calling of his *neshamah* to be revealed, and his real name is a Heavenly ordained hint to that mandate, if not a constant remainder that there is a task to be done and only he can do it.

The Neos Hadesheh writes that the reason one cannot fulfill the mitzvah of counting the Omer simply by listening to his friend count for him (through the concept of *shome'a k'oneh* – one who listens, it's as if he said it), is because the counting of the Omer is a prelude to *Kabbalas haTorah*, which must be unique and exclusive for each and every Jew. Every Jew has his own individual portion in Torah, and his *Kabbalas haTorah* must reflect his acceptance to fulfill his personal requisite. It has been said that there are 600,000 *Yidden*, 600,000 letters in the Torah, and 600,000 interpretations for every verse in the Torah. The very name "Yisrael" is an acronym for "*yesh shishim ribo osios l'Torah* – there are 600,000 letters in the Torah," a composite of 600,000 unique portions, each individually designed.

The Greeks made every attempt to sever this personal relationship that each Jew has with Hashem and the Torah, by issuing a decree: "Write for yourselves on the horn of the ox, *She'ein lachem cheilek* - that you don't have a portion with the G-d of Israel." They decreed that we proclaim on the very instrument we employ to awaken our special inner link and bond to Hashem – the horn of the ox – the *shofar* that we blow on Rosh Hashanah – that we have no special portion in Hashem and His Torah. And, although we defeated the Greeks, the victory was not complete; their influence continues to haunt us to this very day.

Koheles (7:1) tells us: "*Tov shem mishemen tov* – A good name is better than good oil." Torah and *mitzvos* are compared to a candle and a light, as it says, "*For a mitzvah is a candle, and the Torah is light. (Mishlei 6:23)*" A person's soul is likened to a candle as well, as it says, "*Man's soul is Hashem's candle.*" (*Mishlei* 20:27) The Torah itself is called "*tov* – good," as it says, "*For I gave you a good teaching; do not forsake My Torah.*" (*Mishlei* 4:2) With all this, perhaps another explanation can be suggested for the *passuk* in *Koheles*. The word "*mishemen tov*" can be understood not as "better than good oil," but rather, "from good oil." This means to say that a good name comes from good oil, and good oil is one that burns well and produces light – namely, the fuel and fire of Torah and *mitzvos*. A good name, that is, using one's name to actualize his potential and uncover his purpose in life and personal portion in Hashem's Torah, comes from "*shemen tov*" – the brilliant oil and light of the only "*tov*" that exists – the Torah. A Jew must peer deeply into the Torah to identify himself, and then his name will become renown in both this world and the next, as he will have uncovered his unique *shoresh haneshamah* (root of his soul) while striving to equate his earthly image with the spiritual projection of it above.

Between Man and His Fellow Man

Everybody Counts - I Don't Get No Respect

A well-known funnyman once lamented: "When I was young, I didn't get no respect. One winter, I asked my father if I could go ice-skating on the frozen pond." He said, "Why don't you wait until the weather warms up!"

Everyone needs respect. The alternative is catastrophic. Whether it is a child, an adult, a boss or an employee, the need to feel and to know that others respect his existence is as essential as the air we breathe. Indeed, the many times the *Ribono Shel Olam* counted us in the Torah were to emphasize His tremendous love for His people. (*Rashi, Bamidbar* 1:1) We thereby became an accounted-for entity, an entity of distinction, which cannot become *batul b'rov* (nullified by being absorbed into the majority). Whereas in the general world, to be looked at as a number is a consequence of bureaucracy, to be counted by the *Ribono Shel Olam* is an indicator of each Jew's singularity, uniqueness, and special *koach haneshamah*, inner soul and strength.

The Gemara in *Bava Metziah* (85a) teaches a valuable lesson in this regard. Rabbeinu Hakadosh visited the city of Rabbi Elazar Ben Rabbi Shimon after the latter's demise, and was informed that he had left behind a son who had strayed from the path of Torah. Because of this young man's unusual handsomeness and appeal, he was sought out by the promiscuous women of the world, to the point that prostitutes were willing to pay large sums for his attentions. Immediately, Rabbeinu Hakadosh went to meet with him and conferred *semichah* upon him, giving him the title of Rabbi. Having ordained him, he hired Rabbi Shimon Ben Isi as his tutor to teach the young man Torah and to cultivate a relationship with him. Each time the young man was tempted to return to his old way of life, Rabbi Shimon Ben Isi reminded him that someone who wears the cloak of rabbinical distinction is too distinguished to associate with such behavior. Ultimately, the young man persevered, until he became the great Rabbi Yosi ben Rabbi Elazar. It all began with a show of respect.

How perspicacious was the great *tzaddik* of Yerushalayim, Rav Aryeh Levin *zt"l*, who took a young thirteen-year-old orphan into his home! Out of respect for the boy's plight, R' Levin addressed the boy in the third person. This orphan, whom Rav Aryeh built up, eventually became his son-in-law and one of the luminaries of Yerushalayim, Harav Shmuel Aharon Yudelevitch *zt"l*.

The mishnah in *Avos* (2:10, 2:13) enumerates the positive attributes that each of the five *talmidim* of Rabbi Yochanan Ben Zakkai felt were most important. They were:

1) *Ayin tovah* – an attitude of tolerance and benevolence toward others.

2) *Chaver tov* – to be a good friend and to acquire one.

3) *Shachein tov* – to be a good neighbor and to acquire one.

4) *Ro'eh es hanolad* – to foresee the results of one's actions.

5) *Lev tov* – to allow one's heart to be inspired to bestow goodness and kindness upon others.

Upon learning this mishnah, it is immediately evident that the first three attributes and the fifth pertain to a person's personal growth and how it affects others. On the other hand, the fourth one, the *middah* of foreseeing consequences, need not relate to others at all, and simply could be encouraging perception in one's own affairs. It doesn't seem to fit with the other four.

One might suggest that not only does this fourth attribute belong with the rest, but it can be the underlying foundation of all the others. How does a person develop into one who possesses an *ayin tovah* or a *lev tov*, or a person who is a *chaver tov* or a *shachein tov*? Precisely by being a visionary, a *ro'eh es hanolad*, one who has a futuristic view of his friend; one who does not look only at what is visible today, but instead, at what will be born out of that person. The future that he envisions for himself and for his friend is the actualization of mankind's potential, and the resulting chain of effects when that potential is fulfilled.

Harav Shlomo Heiman *zt"l*, the venerable *rosh yeshivah* of Yeshivah Torah Vodaath, once gave a *shiur* to the handful of *bachurim* who had braved that day's heavy snowstorm. Despite the small turnout, he gave the *shiur* with the same energy and powerful delivery as he would have with a larger audience. In explaining as to why he expended so much unnecessary vigor for such a small crowd, the *rosh yeshivah* responded, "I am not speaking to you alone! I am speaking to you, and to your children, and to their children!" He truly was a *ro'eh es hanolad*, a visionary.

Every Jew is unique; every Jew is holy; every Jew is sweet. Let us emulate our Creator by making sure we let each Jew know how much he counts, and by showing him the great respect he deserves.

Giving, Never Taking

A man parked his new Bentley outside of a prestigious Midtown Manhattan bank and rushed in to see a bank official about a loan.

"I'd like to borrow $50,000 as soon as possible," he requested.

"Do you realize that in addition to your responsibility for the loan itself, you will be assuming the repayment of the interest at a high rate for the five years of the terms of this loan, should it be approved?" the clerk inquired.

"Yes! Absolutely!" the man responded.

"Now, do you have something you can use as collateral against the loan?" the bank clerk requested.

"Sure thing!" said the man. "That's my Bentley parked outside. Here are the keys. Take them!"

"Fine, here is your bank check for $50,000," said the clerk. He ordered the security guard to park the car in the bank's underground lot, and the man was on his way.

Just a week later, the man was back with the $50,000 cash plus the interest payment, to the bank clerk's utter surprise.

"If you had the money all along, why would you have bothered taking out the loan in the first place?" the clerk asked.

Handing over the $50,000 debt plus the twenty-five dollars in accumulated interest, the man responded, "Are you kidding? Where else can you get a week's underground parking in Midtown Manhattan for only twenty-five bucks?"

We have become a society of takers and manipulators. The better one maneuvers, the more he advances. Our approach to life has become one of "what's in it for me?" The days of "Ask not what your country can do for you; ask what you can do for your country," have been replaced with stimulus packages and bailouts. Our behavior is a far cry from that of Shmuel Hanavi, who absolutely refused to have any benefit from anyone (see *Brachos* 10), or from the holy *Tanna*, Rabbi Pinchas Ben Yair, for whom Heaven intervened (see *Chullin* 7) to enable him to avoid benefiting from the hospitality of Rabbeinu Hakadosh. The Gemara allows one the prerogative to derive pleasure from others, as Elisha Hanavi did in accepting the hospitality from the *Ishah haShunamis*. Still, though, there is no doubt that Elisha Hanavi did so only on the condition that he could reciprocate many times over (see the *Meiri* in *Brachos* 10).

The reason for these great people's conduct of self-reliance was twofold: Firstly, so as not to become subservient to anyone but Hashem; secondly, so as not to develop the character trait of a "taker," irrespective of whether or not it was at someone else's expense. And although it would be unrealistic to equate ourselves with these great *ba'alei madreigah*, we would be terribly remiss if we allowed ourselves to succumb to the self-serving spirit of the "give me" generation. Unfortunately, this spirit has even penetrated some communities of *bnei* Torah, where once politely requested and much appreciated financial support of parents and in-laws, has now evolved into an expectation, if not a demand. It is a clear manifestation of the *"tzu kumt mir"* attitude which only reflects the "give me" posture of society at large.

My *rebbi*, Harav Shlomo Freifeld *zt"l*, would so passionately point out the greatness of the simple act of the previous generation to always respond to one's greeting of *"A gut morgen* (good morning)" with *"A gut morgen, a gut yahr* (good morning, good year)." Their motive was to ensure that they would always give back more than they received. You were kind enough to wish me a good day; I therefore wish you a good day, too, but in addition, I also "give you" my blessing for a good year. (Of course this could go on forever!)

The story of Rav Preida (*Eiruvin* 54) is an incredible demonstration of giving, and then giving even more. He had a student who had difficulty understanding the lesson. Rav Preida, one of the greatest Tanna'im of his day, took upon himself the responsibility to teach the lesson to this student until he'd finally "get it." Rav Preida proceeded to patiently review each lesson with him four hundred times until the student finally comprehended it. One time, in the course of teaching him, Rav Preida was interrupted with a message that he would be needed imminently for a mitzvah-related matter. He nonetheless continued to teach the lesson over and over again, until he had taught his student the requisite four hundred times. This time, though, the student still did not understand the lesson.

"Why is today different than other days?" Rav Preida asked his student.

The student answered, "Once the message came that the *rebbi* is needed for a mitzvah-related matter, I nervously anticipated that the *rebbi* might leave any minute, and I lost my concentration!"

Undaunted, Rav Preida said to his student, "Try to concentrate now, and I will teach it to you again." He then patiently taught him the material another four hundred times until the student understood. The Gemara concludes that Heaven rewarded Rav Preida for giving so much time to this student, and granted him four hundred more years to his life. When we give, not only do we not lose, but we gain the time and opportunities to give even more.

Indeed, in the introduction to *Teshuvos Chasam Sofer*, the Chasam Sofer writes that one should never think that helping out another Jew by learning with him will decrease his personal time for learning. Such thinking is built on the common distortion that we control our successes in Torah study, when in fact there is *siyata d'Shmaya* (Heavenly assistance) intimately involved (see *Megillah* 6). When one gives of his time, energy, and patience, and learns with others, the *Ribono Shel Olam* guarantees that the diminished amount of time that remains for his personal learning will be blessed with such clarity and lucidity, that it will enable him to stretch himself and accomplish more in less time.

Our *tzaddikim's* "giving" approach to life dates back to Avraham Avinu, who refused to take anything from the king of Sedom, and it has been their creed throughout the generations. In Kelm in the late 1800's, they would auction off various honors for the year on Simchas Torah. However, the bids were not for the honor of *Chassan* Torah or *Chassan Bereishis*, but for the honor to be the one to clean the *beis medrash*, or to kindle the heater, or to light the candles before *davening*. The honor of carrying the washing cup along with the heavy bucket of water, to enable the *kohanim* to have their hands washed before *Birchas Kohanim*, was bought by the Alter of Kelm himself. A young boy named Yerucham (later to become the famed Mirrer *Mashgiach*, Rav Yerucham Levovitz *zt"l*) once saw the Alter *shlepping* the bucket and wanted to relieve him, but the Rosh Yeshivah would not relinquish his hold on it. Clutching the bucket close to him, he said, "Young man! This is an honor I paid for. Please don't take it away from me!" Undoubtedly, such a role model made an indelible impression on this young boy destined to be *mechanech* the next generation.

The well-known story of Rav Moshe Feinstein *zt"l* and the car door is another example of this exemplary *middah* belonging to *chashuve Yidden*. A *bachur* who had given the Rosh Yeshivah a ride reached over to open the door for him and inadvertently slammed the door on Rav Moshe's finger. Although in great pain, Rav Moshe didn't utter a sound. The explanation was simple: This *bachur* was giving to me. I was taking from him. I should dare to make him feel bad for something he did unintentionally, while he was doing me a favor?!

It has been said in the *sefarim hakedoshim* that the very definitions of holiness and impurity are linked to whether one is a giver or a taker. Man's purpose on this world is to give, in order to reveal Hashem's name in the context of the personal world that he builds. Through that effort, he grows in holiness. The person who is absorbed in taking for himself will cave in to the negative *middos* of *ga'avah*, *ta'avah*, and the like, and this will lead to a path of impurity and contamination.

When Rav Yochanan Hasandlar would make a shoe with the calculated intention that it be a strong shoe, a durable shoe, one that would serve its wearer well for many years, it was a "giving" act – and therefore an act of holiness. Compare such thinking with the "take as much as you can" attitude of today's "make to break and discard" manufacturers, and one understands that the impurity has spread way beyond the confines of promiscuity and licentiousness. The self-centeredness of the "taker" is sure to lead to the fragmentation that lies at the core of all that is impure. The greater the disintegration from the Source of all life, the greater the impurity will be.

On the other hand, the more we are "givers," the more we unite the creation, and the more we trace it all back to its one Source, the more progress we are making in a process of holiness. One could readily imagine the difference between a marriage in which both parties are "takers" to one in which both parties focus on giving. In the home of the latter, there is not only peace and tranquility, but the *Shechinah* rests there as well, for the couple's giving nature has made their home a breeding ground for *kedushah*, allowing the *Shechinah* to feel comfortable there.

The blasphemy of the wicked Titus, the general of the Roman army who destroyed the second Beis Hamikdash, caused him to die with an unusual death. A Heavenly Voice rang out that the powerful Titus would be disgraced and destroyed by an insignificant "*bri'ah kalah*," a puny gnat, called disgraceful because it can only ingest but cannot expel. In the name of the Arizal, it is explained why that is so disgraceful: The gnat can only take in, but cannot give, therefore, it is removed from any semblance of holiness. Such is your lot, Titus!

Klal Yisrael is commanded: "*Kedoshim tihiyu* – You shall be holy." How much more so shall we, who are created in the image of Hashem, strive to be among the "givers," as we emulate our Creator and radiate holiness throughout the world.

Emissaries of Hashem

Early one morning, the President surreptitiously slipped out of the White House for his daily jog, without the accompaniment of the Secret Service. Suddenly, a man wearing a ski mask jumped out from behind some bushes with a gun in his hand and screamed out, "Give me all of your money!"

Unwilling to capitulate, the President replied, "You can't do this; I'm the President of the United States of America!"

"Oh!" the thief responded. "Strike that, then. Give me all of <u>my</u> money!"

※

Whose money is it anyway? Truth be told, it's neither mine nor yours, but Hashem's. We are merely His agents, entrusted to carry out the proper transactions. In the investment scandal of 2008-2009, where so many people absorbed major financial losses, a man went to the *gadol* Harav Yosef Shalom Elyashiv *shlit"a* lamenting his loss of a million dollars to this notorious scheme. Instead of the consolation he expected, the great *rav* responded, "Do you mean to say that you had a million dollars in your hands and you held on to it, instead of disbursing it among the many worthy *tzadakah* organizations in need?"

There are numerous stories of *gedolim* who received envelopes with large donations, and before even ascertaining the sum, they gave the entire package to someone who approached them in need. They saw their roles as *shluchei d'Rachmana*, envoys of the *Ribono Shel Olam*, with absolute clarity. There still exist philanthropic Jews today who see their good fortune as a clear directive from Heaven that their task in life is to help distribute the *Ribono Shel Olam's* charities. The tragic events of the 9/11 attack on the World Trade Center, as well as the more recent crash of global markets and universal trust during the fall of 2008, are ample indications that Hashem is sending us a message. A reassessment of our financial fixation and preoccupation is in order.

The well-known adage of "*Tzedakah tatzil mimaves* – charity protects from death *(Mishlei* 10:2*),*" is not only significant because the merit that one earns through his charity provides Heavenly protection from death, but it is to be understood on a practical level as well. If one takes upon himself to act as Hashem's agent in distributing His funds, then longevity is his, because he is an essential part of Hashem's plan. As one of Hashem's employees, his position in life is secure. In this case he acts as an agent of the Source of all life and inevitably draws from that wellspring of life. The *Ribono Shel Olam* welcomes his services for many years to come.

In the *at-bash* coding system (where the first letter of the Hebrew alphabet is substituted for the last, the second for the second to last, etc.), the word "*tzedakah* – charity," is "*tzedakah*" in reverse as well! This is symbolic of the reciprocal way one gains from giving charity. Whatever he gives away, he gains in return. More importantly, as Hashem's special, trusted emissary, he works hand in hand with his Creator, securing his unique relationship with Him for eternity.

Happy With His Portion

Two Irish fellows were walking their dogs one day when they come upon a pub. Finding it difficult not to imbibe, one says to the other, "How about stopping in for a drink?"

The other replies, "We can't go in there like this! Don't you see the sign? 'Absolutely No Pets Allowed!'"

Undeterred, the first guy adjusts his sunglasses, and he and his German shepherd head toward the tavern door.

"Hey! You can't go in there with that dog! Can't you see the sign?" screams the burly bouncer.

"But I'm blind," the man replies, "and this is my seeing-eye dog!"

"I am so sorry!" the bouncer apologizes profusely. "Please go right in and have a drink on the house."

The man's friend, having observed this, tries the same routine. After adjusting his sunglasses, he approaches the tavern door with his dog, only to be stopped by the bouncer.

"Hey, you! You can't go in there with a dog! Can't you see the sign?"

"But I'm blind," the man replies, "and this is my seeing-eye dog."

"Seeing-eye dog?" questions the bouncer. "A Chihuahua?"

"Oh!" said the man. "Is that what they gave me?"

Everyone knows the famous teaching of *Chazal*: "The truly happy person is one who is content with his portion." (*Avos* 4:1) Unfortunately, many people would, in fact, be very happy with "his" (the other fellow's) portion. This is obviously not what *Chazal* had in mind, but rather that one should find contentment in his own particular lot in life. All too often, we focus on what everyone else has and what we lack, instead of appreciating and treasuring our G-d-given uniqueness and purpose. In our nonsensical yearning to be someone else, we lose sight of what Hashem has given us and our singular task on this earth.

It's even worse than that. At times, we can get so caught up and enamored with *yenem's* (the other person's) world, his talents and successes, his celebrations and family dynamics, his capabilities and erudition, that we squander our own world in the process. All we have in the end is the pain of envy and the anguish of disappointment.

And it gets even worse. The Gemara (*Sanhedrin* 106) shares with us the proverbial saying: "The camel went to seek horns for himself, and not only did he not procure horns, but his ears were cut off as well." The saddest part of it all is that the *ba'al kin'ah* loses his own distinct portion in the process and will thereby never actualize the purpose that was his and only his, the accomplishments that nobody else in the world could touch but him. And instead of coming in contact with his *neshamah's* calling and concretizing his vast potential; instead of standing up to the challenges that are unambiguously his, and only his, to hurdle, he surrenders his entire *raison d'etre* for a tradeoff of futility. He will never touch that which was designated for his friend, and he will lose all that was uniquely his own. *Chazal* said it so clearly: "Whoever focuses on that which is not his, whatever he seeks, he never gets, and what he has, is taken away from him." (Sotah 9)

The one who is truly happy with his lot will, in fact, rejoice with his (own) portion *and* be thrilled with his friend's portion. He will be ecstatic about his own special and personal contribution to spreading Hashem's glory during the course of his human experience, and at the same time, he'll be equally exhilarated that his friend, with his unique portion, has the opportunity to accomplish the same.

The Kotzker's *vort* about the words of *Chazal* that, "*Kol haneheneh mi'seudas chassan v'eino mesamcho, oveir b'chamishah kolos* – Whoever derives pleasure from the groom's wedding feast but does not rejoice with him, violates the spirit of the five sounds of joy [mentioned by the prophet]," comes alive. Although typically understood to refer to the attendee of a wedding who doesn't bother attempting to rejoice with the *chassan* and *kallah* with his dancing or encouraging words, the Kotzker explained it differently. He said it refers to one who attends his friend's wedding, and is not overjoyed by his friend's *simchah*. "*V'eino mesamcho*" should be understood as "It doesn't make him happy," referring to the wedding feast not making the *guest* happy. If *yenem's simchah* doesn't make you happy, even if he's a twenty-one-year-old kid, and you're pushing thirty and still single, then you're not truly happy with your lot – not with yours and not with his.

"This above all else – to thy own self be true." That "self" is replete with so much distinctive potential that can build worlds. There is much for which to look forward. There is much reason to rejoice.

Invisible

The nurse barged into the doctor's office.

"Doctor, doctor! You must come immediately! There's a man outside who thinks he's invisible!"

The doctor turned to the nurse.

"Tell him I can't see him right now!"

How often have we walked into a new environment or a strange setting and have felt invisible? No one offered a *"shalom aleichem,"* nobody even gestured a hint of recognition that there was a new face in the crowd. Physically, we knew we existed, but it was as if we were transparent to everyone else in the room. Somehow we faded into oblivion without even trying, simply because we were not from that town. We lost our identity before we even had a chance to identify ourselves. We felt weightless, as if we had no presence. Our "*gut* Shabbos" brought an empty stare, as if we had said something offensive. If the root of the word "*kavod* – honor" is "*kaveid* – heaviness," to feel someone's weight and acknowledge his presence, then this silent treatment is the greatest display of humiliation one could ever imagine.

Ignorance may be bliss, but being ignored is painful and hurtful. All of this pain and hurt could have been averted with two simple words: "*Shalom aleichem.*" A warm greeting, a sensitive word, a welcoming smile – all send a clear message: "You do exist! I recognize your presence!"

The severity of not showing proper *kavod* to one another is hard-hitting and catastrophic. We lost a Beis Hamikdash because of it, twenty-four-thousand students of Rabbi Akiva perished because of it (*shelo nahagu kavod zeh lazeh*), and who knows how many other countless tragedies evolved in its wake. Needless to say, this lack of *kavod* comes in different flavors and stripes and varied levels and realms, but the common thread among all instances of it is a preoccupation with one's self, to the degree that it incapacitates him to see and respect his friend for the noble and prestigious *tzelem Elokim* that he is. That being the case, the person views his fellow man as one who has very little to offer, to the point that he is no more than a disappearing shadow, a mirage at best. *I might have greeted him, but I didn't see anyone there. He really was invisible. I made sure of it!*

The Gemara (*Sanhedrin* 20) tells us that even greater than the Torah-erudite generations of Moshe and Aharon and

Chizkiyahu Hamelech, was the generation of Rabbi Yehuda Bar Ila'i. His was a generation so poor, that there was but one *tallis* (blanket) to cover six students, and nonetheless they persevered and studied Torah with great diligence. The magnitude of this assiduousness seems to lie in their ability to persevere in their *limud haTorah* despite their hardships and dire straits.

Rav Chaim Shmulevitz *zt"l* insightfully explains their greatness in a different light: The likelihood of six people sharing one blanket and each of them being properly covered and enjoying a restful and comfortable respite, is remote, if not impossible. Even one who is most sensitive and kind while awake is likely to be oblivious to everything while asleep, and he will naturally pull the cover in his direction. How special and unique was the generation of Rabbi Yehuda Bar Ila'i; how great was the *kavod* they had for one another; how remarkable was their sensitivity and empathy to feel the presence of one another and ensure each other's comfort, even while asleep!

The Kotzker Rebbe *zt"l* explained the following mishnah in *Avos* in his inimitable style:

"*Shnayim she'yoshvim v'ein beineihem divrei Torah, harei zeh moshav leitzim* – If two are sitting together and there is not between them words of Torah, they are classified as an assembly of fools." (*Avos* 3:3) The Kotzker inserted a comma after the words "*v'ein beineihem* – and there is not between them," and said the following: "*Shnayim sheyoshvim*" – If two Jews sit together in peace and harmony, with mutual love and respect, "*v'ein beineihem*" – and there are no differences between them, but rather they are a mutual admiration society who bestow the greatest of *kavod* upon one another; "*divrei*

Torah" – this show of *kavod* is itself the words of Torah at their best.

It is told that the Chazon Ish *zt"l*, who was an extremely pious and holy person and was most certainly careful to avoid seeing any impure sights, was nonetheless careful to wear his glasses when walking in the street. He feared that otherwise, if he encountered an acquaintance, he might not be cognizant of his presence and therefore not greet him properly. Clearly the importance of *kavod habriyos* – honoring another person – was of paramount importance to him, even in the face of other challenges.

We need to guard our eyes from the obvious negative influences that surround us, yet at the same time, focus them on the perpetual opportunities of visualizing and giving credence and strength to all we encounter. And with this show of *kavod*, we will not only be honoring our friend, but our Creator as well.

Selflessness

A woman calls Mt. Sinai Hospital.

"Hello, I'd like to talk to you about a patient's condition. I want to know *everything* about her condition, from top to bottom. Give me a detailed report."

"That's somewhat of an unusual request," says the operator. "I'll have to connect you to a supervisor."

An authoritative voice comes on the line: "Yes, how can I help you?"

"I'm calling about Sara Finkel in room 302. Can you please give me the details on her condition?"

"Let me see; Farber, Feinberg, Finkel. Yes, here it is, Sara Finkel. She's off the oxygen, she finished her antibiotics, the feeding tube is out, and she's eaten three square meals and looks quite alert.

As a matter of fact, the doctor says that if she keeps improving, he's going to send her home on Tuesday."

The woman on the other end is ecstatic. "Oh! Thank G-d! That's wonderful! That's great news! I am so happy to hear that! She's going home already on Tuesday! That's marvelous!"

The supervisor responds, "Ma'am, from your genuine concern and enthusiasm, I assume you must be a very dear friend or relative."

"Dear friend or relative?" the woman says. "This is Sara Finkel!! My doctor don't tell me nothing!"

If we would be concerned about others as much as we are concerned about ourselves, that would be quite an achievement. To be sensitive to another person at our own expense is an even greater accomplishment. When it involves being *ma'avir al middosav* – giving up what one justly deserves in favor of another, it is an act that brings enormous *nachas* and enjoyment to the *Ribono Shel Olam*.

Such was the selflessness of Rachel Imeinu. Out of concern for her sister Leah's embarrassment, she gave away the *simanim* – signs – that she and Yaakov Avinu had agreed upon in order to expose her father Lavan's deception. Not only did she relinquish her husband-to-be and potentially her future as a matriarch of Klal Yisrael, not only did she absorb the embarrassment of not being the bride at her own wedding and risk incurring the wrath of a disappointed *chassan*, she even lowered herself to hide under the bed during the course of an intimacy that rightfully was hers, so she could respond to Yaakov's call, so that Leah's voice would not be detected (*Pesichta D'Eicha Rabbasi*). It was this *mesiras nefesh* – self sacrifice – that stands at the core of

Rachel Imeinu's ongoing prayer and cry that her children return from the painful exile. It is this altruism that makes her *tefillos* so penetrating that Hashem responds (*Yirmiyahu* 31:16-17), *"Hold back your voice from wailing, and your eyes from tears, for there is reward for your intercession,"* Your prayers will be answered. *"[Klal Yisrael] will return from the land of the enemy. There is hope in the end; your children will return to their borders."* Indeed, to this day, thousands flock to Kever Rachel, Rachel's tomb, to daven that Rachel Imeinu continue to intercede on behalf of her children by virtue of the eternal merit of her epic self-sacrifice. Such is the great merit of a *maavir al middosav*.

The unflinching love between Dovid and Yehonasan is described by Dovid Hamelech, as he laments his devoted friend's demise (*Shmuel II*, 1:26), as "more wondrous than the love of women." Haramah Mipano (*Ma'amar Chakor Din* 4:17) explains this peculiar metaphor as a reference to two particular women in the history of Klal Yisrael, our matriarchs Rachel and Leah. That Yehonasan ben Shaul could be so prepared to abdicate the throne in favor of his best friend, without a trace of envy and with absolute determination to become his trusted servant, was a *yerushah*, a bequest from the love of those particular women, Rachel and Leah. Rachel had infused selflessness into the bloodstream of her descendents, enabling Yehonasan to rise to the occasion (since Yehonasan was from the tribe of Binyamin, son of Rachel).

This *middah*, character trait, is precious indeed, and presents an auspicious opportunity. *Chazal* tell us (*Rosh Hashanah* 17a), "When one waives his rights in favor of another, the *Ribono Shel Olam* in turn forgives all of his sins." The logic is simple.

If one can let things pass that, according to the letter of the law, are legitimately his, Hashem can ignore the letter of the law in his favor. It works with the classic rule of Heavenly judgment, *middah k'neged middah,* which states that Heaven deals with a person the way he deals with others. Taken seriously, a vilification can turn into a golden opportunity; a maligning into a favorable circumstance. The result is a clean record and a purity of heart that makes one's *tefillos* more potent and engaging, as the power of Rachel crying for her children, *Rachel mevakah al banehah,* becomes his own.

There is a story told of a bar mitzvah *bachur* who, in spite of having spent a long time preparing the *leining* of his *parshah,* allowed another bar mitzvah *bachur* to *lein* that Shabbos in his stead. As a result of a miscalculation on the part of the gabbai of the shul, both had been scheduled to read the Torah the same week. Four years later, the boy's mother was hospitalized with a serious heart condition, and the boy stayed with her in the hospital over Shabbos. A man came into her hospital room that Shabbos morning, trying to recruit a *minyan* of people to pray with a venerable *rav* who was hospitalized as well. The man asked if the young teenager could possibly read the Torah. Being that it happened to be *Parshas Beshalach,* his bar mitzvah *parshah,* the boy readily agreed. The ailing *rav* was none other than the *gadol* Harav Yosef Shalom Elyashiv, *shlita,* who thanked the young man for *leining* so beautifully. Upon learning of the boy's mother's illness, Rav Elyashiv insisted that his own world-renowned cardiologist consult on the case. Through that doctor's insightfulness and medical expertise, the woman's life was saved. No doubt the legacy of Rachel Imeinu served this selfless *bachur* well, and the *Ribono Shel Olam* responded in kind.

We must remember that we, too, can employ that piercing cry of Rachel Imeinu, when we, like her, are forgiving and selfless for the sake of others. We must always remember the teaching of *Chazal* (*Taanis* 22a): A person should try to be *rach kakaneh* – soft and pliable like a reed that blows in the wind, able to adjust to different conditions, and capable of bending, flexing, and twisting without breaking. When one uses this *middah* to benefit others, the pleasure that it brings the *Ribono Shel Olam* is immeasurable, and the blessings from *Shamayim* are sure to follow.

That's His Problem

Harry was a chronic worrier. He was always tense and nervous. Nothing could calm his incessant neurosis. His friends knew him as "Harry the worrier."

One day, Harry's friends noticed a dramatic change in him. He was relaxed and laid-back, seemingly without a care in the world.

"Harry! What happened to you? You look great. You're like a new person!" they complimented him.

"Well," said Harry, "I don't worry anymore. I hired a professional worrier to worry for me for $1000 a week. Since then I haven't had a single since."

"Harry! $1,000 a week? How are you going afford to pay him?" his friends asked.

"Pay him?" said Harry. "That's his problem!"

How many times do we shirk our responsibility to the needs of the community by saying, "Oh, that's someone else's problem, and I need not concern myself with it"? Were everyone to rationalize this way, nothing would ever be accomplished. *Baruch* Hashem for those courageous few who assume responsibility and dedicate themselves with *mesiras nefesh* to the needs of Klal Yisrael.

In the *Yekum Purkan* prayer on Shabbos morning, we beseech Hashem to bless *"v'chol mi she'oskim b'tzarchei tzibbur b'emunah* – all those who are involved in the needs of the community with faith." The added expression of *"b'emunah* – with faith," seems unnecessary and out of place. What does faith in Hashem have to do with it?

In truth, though, it's all about faith in Hashem. To embark upon a project for the sake of the *klal* demands an absolute belief in *siyata d'Shmaya*, that through one's *"issarusa d'lisata* – exuberance from below (this world)," one will merit *"issarusa d'lieila* – inspiration from Above," which will carry him through. On paper, it may make no sense. One doesn't have the time, the funding, or the energy. Nonetheless, if he has the willpower, and the firm belief that those who assume responsibility will be given the strength and the means from the *Ribono Shel Olam*, then his courage will meet with success. There isn't an organization of Torah or *chessed* in the world that didn't begin with the conviction and vision of a few believers and a surge of *siyata d'Shmaya*.

This lesson can be learned from Yehuda, who offered to forfeit his portion in the World to Come, his most precious commodity, and assumed the responsibility for the safe return of his brother Binyamin. There is a well-known *vort* of the Gaon on the words: "*Vayigash eilav Yehuda vayomer 'Bi adoni...'* – And Yehuda approached him (Yosef) and he said, 'Please, my master...'" (*Bereishis* 44:18) The *trup* (cantillation) for these words has a meaning of its own that actually explains why Yehuda, the fourth son, and not Reuven, the eldest, approached Yosef with the impassioned plea to let Binyamin go free. The cantillation for these words is "*kadma v'azla rivi'i, zarka munach sagol,*" which, when translated literally, can mean: The fourth son preceded the others, because he had relinquished his treasured portion in the world of eternity [as a guarantee to his father for Binyamin's safe return].

Can any of us ever imagine giving up the fortune we amassed over time for the sake of a cause, let alone giving up our eternity for it? Yet Yehuda accepted the responsibility, and it was that merit, writes Rav Shimon Schwab *zt"l*, in the name of his *rebbi*, Rav Yosef Leib Bloch *zt"l*, which earned him a rush of energy and confidence, a *siyata d'Shmaya* that allowed the up-until-now respectful and subservient Yehuda to speak to the king (Yosef) with such directness and tenacity.

Rav Chaim Shmulevitz *zt"l* once said that the world mistakenly thinks that one who is successful is *b'simchah* (happy), when conversely, the one who is *b'simchah* is successful. True *simchah* – happiness – is defined by virtue of growth. The word "*simchah*" itself is rooted in the word *tzemichah* – growth. If a person's relationship with Hashem is growth-oriented and developing, if he is nurturing a closeness and intimacy with

Him, if the person's *ratzon* (will) has created a *tzinor* – a pipe, a conduit ("*tzinor*" has the same letters as "*ratzon*") that connects him with Hashem, then he will truly be *b'simchah*, and success will be his.

The connection between the one involving himself in the community's needs and faith in Hashem is clear. One's success in doing things for the *klal* is most definitely contingent upon his closeness with Hashem. The more he trusts in that relationship, the less he has to fear, for no doubt, Hashem will reward his efforts with tremendous *siyata d'Shmaya*.

Let us make an effort to always make "his problem," ours, and *Hakadosh Baruch Hu* will undoubtedly make all of our problems His, with a lot of *siyata d'Shmaya*, amen.

We'll Leave the Light On for You

A man walks into the office of a cardiologist and says, "Excuse me, Doctor, I have a big problem. I think I am a moth."

The doctor berates him: "Listen! I'm a busy man. I'm not a psychiatrist; I'm a cardiologist. I'm sure you saw the sign on the door. Why did you come in here in the first place?"

"Oh, I don't know," the man says. "I guess I just saw the light on, so I came right in!"

In the darkness of *Olam Hazeh* which prevails so heavily upon us today, people are eager to find a little *"lichtigkeit,"* warmth and encouragement, to get them through their day. Motel 6 knows quite well how attractive their slogan "We'll leave the light on for you" is to the lonely traveler on the dark highway. And indeed all of us, traversing the complex paths of life, are in need of the support and security of something bright and gleaming.

There are those who suffer from a psycho-physiological disorder r"l in which their moods are affected by the lack of sunlight. For these people, winter is horrific, and during that season, despondency dominates. In truth, whose mood is not vastly improved on a sunny day, or by a change in the coldness of the winter to a milder climate? So many migrate to Florida or California to spend their winter break in a more welcoming atmosphere.

The Gemara (*Taanis* 22) tells us how Eliyahu Hanavi appeared to the *chachamim* and pointed out two men, saying, "They are destined to be members of the World to Come."

Curious as to why these two men were worthy of such an accolade, the *chachamim* approached them and asked what their profession was.

The two men replied, "We are jesters, and we bring cheer to those who are despondent."

Rashi explains their term "*semeichim* – we are happy people," as "*u'misamchim bnei adam* – and we make others happy." How magnificent is the *zechus* of one who brings light to others!

Every person possesses this talent. Hashem blessed us all with the ability to smile. A smile nourishes. It does to a person what sunshine does to a plant. A good word, a compliment, a "*yasher koach*," a bit of encouragement, a pat on the back, a warm "*shalom aleichem*," putting forth the effort to remember someone's name or situation – all of these acts are much-needed boosts of energy to a person, and are like infusions of nutrition for him.

Chazal underscore the significance of this lesson in their comment on the blessing that Yaakov Avinu gave to Yehuda: "*Your eyes will be red from the abundance of wine, and your teeth will be white from the abundance of milk.*" (*Bereishis* 49:12) They comment: "It need not be understood exclusively as 'your teeth will become white from milk,' but can be understood as 'the flashing of the whiteness of one's teeth (one's "magic smile"), which is more nourishing than milk.'" (The prefix "*mei*" in *meichalav* can be interpreted as "more than", instead of "from".)

Jews need to be *mechazeik*, to encourage, one another and, without exception, they have the talent to do so. The Gemara (*Shabbos* 89) makes this unequivocally clear. When Moshe Rabbeinu ascended to Heaven to receive the Torah, he found Hashem attaching crowns to specific letters of the *sefer* Torah, and respectfully remained silent. The *Ribono Shel Olam*, disturbed, as it were, by Moshe's silence, asked, "Moshe, don't they teach the practice of saying "*shalom aleichem*" back from where you come?"

Moshe Rabbeinu responded that he didn't think it would be respectful for a servant to initiate a greeting to his Master.

Hashem responded, "[At the very least,] you should have assisted Me," which Rashi explains to mean: "You should have said, '*Titzlach b'melachtecha* – have success in Your endeavor.'"

If we are to be "*mechazeik*" Hashem, Who doesn't need our *chizuk*, surely we must be *mechazeik* one another, especially when we are so desperately reliant on such warmth and encouragement. We do not fulfill our obligation of being kind to one another by saying "*shalom aleichem*" in the *tefillah* of *Kiddush Levanah*. The *Ribono Shel Olam* felt this matter important enough to make mention of it in the midst of Moshe receiving the Torah.

Let us, therefore, make a major effort to use the *kochos* with which Hashem has blessed us, to emulate Him as the quintessential reviver and encourager, and bring "*lichtigkeit*" to others. In doing so, we will have fulfilled "Just as He nourishes and nurtures, so shall you; just as He gives light, so shall you!"

Festivals

Elul – Teshuvah: How Will I Ever Get There?

Sam was over an hour late for work again and his boss called him to task.

"Sam! What happened to you today? It's past 10:00. You're late!"

"It's not my fault! The weather outside is wild! Rain, sleet, snow, slush; you name it! Why, for every step I took forward, I slipped two steps backwards!"

"Sam," his irate boss responded, losing his patience, "if every time you took one step forward, you went two steps backwards, how in the world did you ever get here?"

"It was simple. Eventually, I just turned around to go home!"

―※―

The most difficult aspect of many tasks is not the undertaking itself, but initiating it. It's hard to get started. "*Kol haschalos kashos* – All beginnings are hard." (*Tosfos, Taanis* 10b) Whether it is our natural laziness, or a fear of failure, somehow, we manage to procrastinate and delay getting started on even the simplest chores. When something is unpleasant, it becomes even harder; and there is nothing more difficult than facing one's indiscretions.

The *Ribono Shel Olam*, in His great benevolence, not only graced us with the gift of *teshuvah*, but He reaches out to us from every direction to help us begin the process. He beckons to us: "*Seek out the Hashem when He is to be found; call out to Him when He is close by.*" (*Yeshayahu* 55:6) He entreats us: "I'm here, I'm available, I am welcoming and I am warm; and I eagerly await your return."

And He says, "I know it's hard to start. Simply make a small gesture, a minute show of inspiration, and I will expand upon it. I will bond our relationship from within; I will create a grandiose response of inspiration from Above." In the words of *Chazal*: "You make a small opening like one made by the point of a needle, and I (Hashem) will expand that opening to the size of the entrance to a grand ballroom." (*Medrash Tanchuma, Toldos* 18) As the Kotzker *zt"l* once said (related by R' Shlomo Freifeld *zt"l*): "Where is the *Ribono Shel Olam*? Wherever you let Him in!"

The Mezritcher Maggid says regarding the well-known *Chazal*, "*Yeish koneh olamo b'sha'ah achas* – Sometimes, a person acquires his entire reward in [only] one hour," that the word "*sha'ah*," which usually means "hour," need not be interpreted as an element of time but as a physical motion. It could mean "to turn," as the *passuk* in *Bereishis* (4:5), in describing Hashem's reaction to the offering of Kayin, says: "*V'el Kayin v'el minchaso lo sha'ah* – And to Kayin and to his offering He (Hashem) did not turn." Using this definition of the word "*sha'ah*," Chazal are teaching us that sometimes a person can acquire his eternity with one turn in the right direction, or by turning away from the wrong direction.

With a small turn toward the *Ribono Shel Olam*, a person can merit a massive response, a monolithic surge of *siyata d'Shmaya*, a monumental flow of inspiration from Above; a small step for a man, but yet a giant leap for his *neshamah*. All one has to do is simply turn around to go home.

Rosh Hashanah – Teshuvah: Return to Your Essence

Matt, a young, aspiring, Jewish actor from Long Island, had made the long trek to Hollywood against his parents' better wishes. He, like so many others, was convinced that he had what it takes to make it as a leading man, only to discover that there was little interest in his supposed talent. After months of disappointment, during which he took many different menial jobs just to get by, he was about to give up and go home. As a last resort, he decided to take one last crack at the classifieds. There it was; an immediate opening for an actor! It was only after he circled the ad that he noticed that the role they were looking to fill was an ape.

It wasn't exactly what he had in mind, but at that point, he couldn't be picky.

When he arrived at the interview, he was further disillusioned. It wasn't a film production company. It was the local zoo. The zoo had spent so much money on renovations to create a natural-looking habitat that it could no longer afford to import the ape they needed from Africa. They had no choice but to hire an actor to play the role.

After accepting the job, Matt's conscience kept nagging him. He was being dishonest, fooling the crowd who had paid to see a real ape. In addition, he felt like a fool, dressed in his monkey costume; a failure and a fraud. But after a few days on the job, he was amused by the attention of the crowd, and began to put on a show; hanging upside-down from the branches by his legs, swinging about on the vines, climbing up and down the cage walls, and roaring with all his might as he beat his chest. Soon, he was drawing a sizeable crowd.

One day, a large group of school kids came to see the popular ape. Spurred on by the large audience, Matt climbed a little too far. Twisting over the cage wall; he tumbled into the neighboring lion's den. Terrified, Matt backed up as far as he could from the carnivorous beast. He feared that it was all over. He vaguely remembered from his scant Hebrew School education that at times like this you say the Shema, so he covered his eyes and screamed at the top of his lungs, "*Shema Yisrael, Hashem Elokeinu Hashem echad!*"

The lion, almost upon him, opened its powerful jaws and roared, "*Baruch Shem k'vod malchuso l'olam va'ed!*"

From a nearby cage, a panda yelled, "Shah! You *shlemiels*! You'll get all of us fired!"

Inside every Jew is a beautiful *neshamah*, a soul begging for expression. At times, it is buried so deeply and in so well-disguised a manner, that only a dire emergency can bring it to the surface. When it is finally tapped, it can burst forth with remarkable fire and energy, and the Jew will find that suddenly the yoke of Heaven is upon him. In *teshuvah,* the process of repentance and return, it is precisely with this massive spiritual force that we hope to return. We attempt to come in contact with the *chelek Eloka mima'al,* that portion of godliness from above, which lies within every Yid.

Unfortunately, to many, the concept of *teshuvah* conjures up negative thoughts, founded on the inability to deal with past failures. Instead of appreciating it as one of the greatest gifts that *Hakadosh Baruch Hu* has given to mankind (*Sha'arei Teshuvah, sha'ar harishon*), it has become associated with the unpopular themes of chastisement, confession, and regret, ignoring its true essence. Instead of focusing on a uniquely positive experience of rebirth, rejuvenation, actualization of potential, growth, contentment, happiness, and joy, we throw our hands up in the air and surrender to our worst enemy, despair. (The relinquishing of hope is a *yi'ush* – despair – that, in the homiletic sense, can certainly be dubbed *yi'ush shelo mida'as,* despair that results from a misunderstanding of what *teshuvah* is all about.)

Let us understand that in the darkness of *Olam Hazeh,* the physical world, which champions immorality and licentiousness, despotism and anarchy, and debauchery of every conceivable color and shade, there is one area of decay that supersedes all others, and that is the area of *yi'ush,* despair. It implants negativity at its best, and the loss of perspective and dignity. It is antithetical to the *tzuras ha'adam,* the true dimensions of man as intended. It threatens the very core of what an *adam,* should be. The word *adam* in Hebrew contains the very same letters as the word *me'od* (much or very). This implies that man's essence can stretch and expand to transcend and exceed the limitations of this world, as he connects to an omnipotent source that can lift him from the pit of destruction and allow him to soar to unfathomable heights (Maharal, *Derech Chaim* on *Avos*, 1:2). A real man has no place within himself for hopelessness and despair. An *adam*, a person who holds on to his uniquely human potential, understands that *teshuvah* is about yearning and greatness. It is about returning to one's roots, to one's essence, to one's life-source. It is a return to the godliness within, with which he was created.

Indeed, the Rambam writes in *Hilchos Teshuvah* (7:6): "*Gedolah teshuvah* – *teshuvah* is great because it brings one close to the *Shechinah*." On a superficial level, this statement extols the greatness of *teshuvah*, since one who was distant can become beloved and endeared to the *Ribono Shel Olam* once again. Perhaps, though, the Rambam is not only telling us the ultimate result of *teshuvah*, but the course of action as well. *Teshuvah* is a process that is achieved through utilization of the godly form with which people are endowed, reconnecting to the *Shechinah* within oneself, and reaching therein to actualize one's potential for greatness. Its essence is that it brings one closer with the *Shechinah* within. Its greatness lies in the close proximity and availability of that eternal source of light.

Our problem is that our view of reality is myopic and twisted. The physical domain, *gashmius* and material things, are viewed as concrete, while the *ruchnius*, the spiritual domain, is viewed as abstract. In truth, reality lies in the realm of *ruchnius*. Rav Dessler *zt"l* points out on the *passuk* in *Tehillim* (126:1) that invokes the days of Mashiach: "*B'shuv Hashem es shivas Tzion* – when Hashem will return the captivity of Zion", and clarity of vision will reign; we will realize that, "*hayinu k'cholmim*" – we *were* living in a dream world. (And although the plain meaning of that *passuk* appears to discuss the future, nonetheless it does not say we *will* become aware that we are dreamers, rather we *were* dreamers, *hayinu k'cholmim*, in the past tense.) Our entire past, which emphasized the physical, will be seen for the abstraction that it was, and we will finally become aware that reality lies in the realm of *ruchnius*.

Our downfall is our inability to perceive that our *neshamah* is real, and that the G-dly form in which we were created is no less concrete than our hand or our foot or the face we see in the mirror. If only we would recognize that we are literally connected to the *Ribono Shel Olam* through this G-dly form, and we would view the world through the lens of *emes* – truth, we would readily understand how natural it is to return to that which is our true essence. We would run to return with tremendous yearning and energy to the *Ribono Shel Olam,* to Whom we are intimately and eternally bound.

"*Hashiveinu Hashem eilecha v'nashuvah* – return us, Hashem, to You, and we will return." (Eichah 5:21) Return us, Hashem, to You, to the godliness within, to our innate G-dly form, to the genuine potential of *adam*, to the real me. And then, having reconnected to our true essence, *v'nashuvah*, we will return to You, Hashem – an all-enveloping return, in the most natural way.

Shabbos Shuvah – You Make Your Own Lunch

Mario and Antonio, two proud Italian-Americans, worked as construction workers on a high-rise project in the heart of Manhattan. Everyday at noon, they would stop their work for their lunch break and they would compare notes.

"Hey, Antonio, whata you gotta for luncha today?" Mario yelled out one day.

"I donna know. I gotta looka ina mya luncha box," replied Antonio. Antonio opened his lunch box and took out a gourmet lunch of pasta salad and pepperoni pizza, with lasagna saturated with Mama Mia's ravioli spaghetti sauce, and a slice of *kishka* with a pastrami sandwich to boot.

"Heya, Mario, whata you gotta for luncha?" asked Antonio

"I donna know. I gotta looka ina mya luncha box," Mario responded. Mario opened his lunch box and much to his dismay, he had tuna fish for lunch.

"I cannota believe it. I gotta tuna fisha fora lunch! And not justa tuna fisha, buta chunka lighta tuna fish! I cannota standa tuna fisha!"

The next day at lunchtime, once again Mario asked Antonio what he had for lunch.

"I donna know! I gotta looka ina mya luncha box."

Antonio pulls out an epicurean luncheon fit for a king of linguini steeped in melted mozzarella cheese, baked ziti, fresh zucchini, potato *borekes*, and mashed potatoes mixed with *schmaltz* and fried onions, with a large slice of Boston cream pie for dessert.

"Whata you gotta for luncha, Mario?"

"I donna know. I gotta looka ina mya luncha box." Once again to his disappointment it's chunk-light tuna fish. "I cannota believe it! Againa chunka lighta tuna fish! I hate tuna fish! I cannota standa this anymore! Tomorrow ifa I havea tuna fisha fora luncha I'ma gonna killa myself! I'ma gonna jumpa offa thisa constructiona site!"

The next day when it was time for lunch, the two engaged in their usual conversation, and once again Antonio plucked out of his lunch-box what would be the envy of every restaurateur in Little Italy.

"Hey, Mario! Whata you gotta for luncha today?"

"I dunno know! I gotta looka ina mya luncha box," Mario replied. Mario opens his lunch box, and lo and behold, it's tuna fish again; soggy chunk-light tuna fish.

"I cannota beara thisa anymore!" he screams out. And in his frustration and despair, Mario walks to the edge of the construction site, hundreds of feet above the ground and is about to jump off to his death, when his friend, Antonio, calls out to him.

"Mario! Don'ta jump! Don'ta killa youraself! Why don'ta you justa tella youra wife thata you don'ta likea tuna fish?"

"Tella mya wife? Whata you say?" Mario exclaimed. "I'ma notta married. I makea mya owna lunch!"

There are auspicious moments in life, when we come to the realization that we can neither blame nor rely upon anyone else, but must rather assume full responsibility for our lives and our future. One of those occasions is Shabbos Shuvah, when the holy day of Yom Kippur is swiftly approaching, and our lives are hanging in the balance. It finally dawns upon us that indeed we make our own lunch; we affect our own destiny, and we need to put our house in order.

The Gemara in *Avodah Zarah* (17a) makes this point abundantly clear as it describes such a turning point and the *teshuvah* that resulted in its wake. Elazar Ben Durdaya was a notorious hedonist, who is described as having met with every harlot in the world. He journeyed across seven rivers to reach a distant city in order to meet up with yet one more. As they were engaged in intimacy, he was suddenly stricken by something she said, and decided to repent with all his heart and soul. He begged the mountains, the heavens and earth, the sun and the moon, and the stars and constellations to intercede on his behalf, but they all refused. Finally, he came to the realization that, "*Ein hadavar talui ela bi* – The matter rests with no one but me!" He cried with such great anguish, that his soul departed from him. As he died, a Heavenly voice rang out; declaring that Rabbi

Elazar Ben Durdaya was designated for eternity. He acquired his Heavenly reward (and the title of Rabbi) in a very brief period of time, evoking the proverbial cry of Rabbeinu Hakadosh of, "*Yeish koneh olamo b'sha'ah achas* – Sometimes, a person acquires his entire reward in [only] one hour!"

One might ask how it is possible for one who is so entrenched in licentiousness and lewd behavior to do *teshuvah* so quickly and efficiently. How can a lifetime of debauchery dissipate in a few short moments? It seems to defy all the laws of nature, that events which occurred can never be undone. *Teshuvah* seems to transcend the typical parameters of time, allowing the past to not only be forgotten, but completely uprooted.

This is precisely the case! *Teshuvah* is one of the wonders of the world. It preceded the creation of the world, and it does not conform to its laws of nature. It has the miraculous ability to not only undo the events of the past as if they never occurred, but it can even turn previous misdeeds into something they were not – positive merits. It is reminiscent of the concept of *hataras nedarim*, when unwarranted vows are erased as if they never were. It is no wonder that both Rosh Hashanah and Yom Kippur are introduced by the nullification of vows through the observance of *hataras nedarim* on *erev* Rosh Hashanah and the *Kol Nidrei* prayer that ushers in Yom Kippur, the holiest day of the year. It is to remind us of the wonder of *teshuvah,* which calls to us to make the attempt to acquire our world of reward *b'sha'ah achas,* in a brief moment.

This phenomenon is underscored by the Gemara in *Kiddushin* (49b). The Gemara proposes that if a man says to a woman, "I marry you on the condition that I am a *tzaddik* (a righteous person)," then even if he was a *rasha* (a sinful person), the marriage is possibly valid. The explanation given for this novel halachah is because perhaps the man had a thought of repentance in mind when he said these words. Is it not amazing what one could accomplish in a fleeting moment of truth?

The Ramban explains that the *passuk* in *Parshas Nitzavim* (*Devarim* 30:11) of, "*This mitzvah that I command you today is not removed from you, nor too distant,*" is referring to the mitzvah of *teshuvah*. However, the choice of words, "*lo nifleis hi* – it is not removed,*"* with the word "*nifleis*" meaning removed, is somewhat troubling. This is because the word "*nifleis*" also has a connotation of "wonder," which could render the translation: "it (*teshuvah*) is not wondrous."

Perhaps it can be suggested that the placement of the word "*mimcha* – from you," immediately following "*lo nifleis hi,*" rather than at the end of the *passuk,* is the key to the resolution of our quandary. Of course *teshuvah* is a *peleh*, a miraculous phenomenon that transcends the limitations of time and nature. But, "*Lo nifleis hi mimcha*" – *teshuvah* is no more a wonder, no more miraculous than *you*, members of Klal Yisrael, are! As part of Klal Yisrael, you are blessed with a gift of resilience that eludes and defies the limitations of the natural world.

It is the power of "*mimcha,*" from you; from within, writes Reb Chaim Volozhiner *zt"l* in *Nefesh Hachaim* (*sha'ar 1, perek 4, hagah*), that can affect worlds way beyond this one. The words to the mishnah in *Avos* hint to this concept. The mishnah says, "*Da mah l'ma'alah mimcha* - Know that what occurs above, is from you," meaning, as a result of your actions. What a winning combination it is: the supernatural power of *teshuvah*, coupled with the supernatural power of a Jew! The wonder of *teshuvah* in conjunction with the wonder of every Jew's gift of *hischadshus* – renewal, is indeed a wonder of wonders, *pilei pla'im*.

No matter how far removed, no matter how far one has strayed, the wonder of *teshuvah* is real and accessible. This is especially so when a Jew comes in contact with his true being. In the words of Rabbi Elazar Ben Durdaya, "The matter rests with no one but me!" This matter of *teshuvah* is contingent upon connecting to oneself, for then, in a harmonious blend, the Jew will defy nature and turn back the clock in the most magnificent and glorious way, and return to Hashem. Then he will have lived up to the words of the prophet, "*Shuva Yisrael ad Hashem Elokecha.*"

Yom Kippur – Teshuvah: Coming Home

A man badly in need of a diet was told by his doctor that if he were to walk five miles a day, he would lose a pound a day.

The man took the doctor's words to heart, and followed his advice. Two months later, the man woke up his doctor in the middle of the night with an emergency phone call.

"Hello, Doc! I want you to know that I did precisely as you said. I walked five miles a day for the past sixty days, and just like you predicted, I've lost sixty pounds!"

"That's wonderful!" responded the doctor. "But why did you have to wake me up at 3:00 in the morning? What's the emergency?"

"You don't understand," the man answered. "I'm 300 miles away from home!"

At times, we attempt to do something spiritually positive, and then it backfires, leaving us fallen in the dust, further away from our goal than when we started. We tried to do *teshuvah*, to discipline ourselves, based on our understanding of the *teshuvah* process, only to feel more remote and distant from Hashem. We had wanted to achieve the desired result of closeness to Hashem, and instead we ended up despondent and disappointed. We had hoped to merit the gracious gift of the *Ribono Shel Olam* to the sincere *baal teshuvah*, that our *zedonos*, our intentional misdeeds, could be transformed into *zechuyos*, merits (*Yoma* 86a). Instead, we fell into a depression about the enormity of our sins, believing deep down that Hashem must hate us and therefore wants nothing to do with us. We thought that we'd finally come home, but instead we found ourselves miles away. Where did we go wrong?

What we've done was, rather than grasp the true meaning of *teshuvah*, we've distorted it, and allowed the *yetzer hara*, the evil inclination, to take us for yet another ride.

Instead of appreciating the *Yamim Nora'im*, the High Holidays, as an amazing act of kindness from Hashem, a golden opportunity to start anew, we fall into the malaise of living in the past, too frightened to face the future, and oblivious of the propitious opportunity of the present. We remain pitifully unaware of the metamorphosis that could take place, if only we allow it. We are ignorant of the transformation that could allow our well-masked yet pristine *neshamah tehorah*, innocent soul, to surface, and subvert our overindulged personae. The spiritual side of us could soar, while our earthly side would bow its shameful head.

It depends very much on our mindset and self-image. Years ago, a sign on the wall toward the exit of the monkey-house in the Bronx Zoo read: "World's most dangerous animal. World's greatest predator. This creature preys on tens of thousands of other creatures which are vulnerable to it." Which dreadful beast could this be? And why was the sign next to a mirror rather than a cage? The implication of the sign's message was clear; the animal is the human race. People are nothing more than another species of animal. This is what you are all about. You might as well act the part. You'll never escape the reality of your limited existence. Come join the zoo club. Live in a cage, and eat all you can!

Such thinking is not only antithetical to the *teshuvah* process, it is spiritually suicidal. There is a reason why Rosh Hashanah, which is very the day of judgment, is nonetheless devoid of *vidui*, confession, which is instead pushed off to Yom Kippur. Surely, one would think that the prayers for Rosh Hashanah, the day of judgment, should be filled with heartfelt expression of self-reproach and remorse. Why is there no *ashamnu* confession on Rosh Hashanah; no chest-beating, no *al cheit*, no extended self-chastisement; only talk of crowning Hashem as the king? Isn't Yom Kippur a little late for intense introspection?

The answer to the above question, in truth, underscores the very foundation of *teshuvah*. Only after the invigorating experience of *romemus*, exaltedness that Rosh Hashanah affords us, are we open to the purification process of Yom Kippur. Only after proclaiming and crowning Hashem as *Melech Malchei Hamelachim*, the King Who rules over all other monarchs, with the implication that as His constituents, we are worthy members of a *mamleches kohanim v'goy kadosh (Shemos 19:6)*, a kingdom of priests and a holy nation, and therefore the nobility and aristocracy of humanity, are we energized to face the details of our inadequacies, with a perspective of our *gadlus hamoach* and *romemus hanefesh,* importance and the exaltedness of our souls. Only after a display of absolute recognition that the Master of the Universe is the One Who, in the words of *Tehillim* (113:7-8), *"Raises the needy from the dust, the poor from the trash heaps, to seat them with the nobles, the nobles of His people,"* with full cognizance that no matter how far one has strayed, the *Ribono Shel Olam* is always ready to lift him up and seat him among the elite, can we face the music on Yom Kippur. Only after having realigned himself with *Malchus Shamayim,* the Kingdom of Heaven, thereby regaining his confidence in the warm, extended hand of the *Ribono Shel Olam,* will one be properly equipped to engage in a *teshuvah* process. This way, although the process may twinge and sting; it will not depress and destroy. Instead it will produce a new creation, a refreshed, rejuvenated, and vibrant servant of Hashem; a proud member of the nation of the King. No longer will he feel estranged, for he has finally come home.

Yom Kippur – Ne'ilah: Help Me Stop Stealing

People from New York get a bum rap. I don't know why they have a reputation that they are self-centered and unhelpful. Why just the other day, I observed two New Yorkers sharing a cab. One guy was taking the battery, and the other guy was taking the tires!

Although we might be guilty of many minor indiscretions, most of us are not hard-nosed criminals. We have our problems with the challenges of *kin'ah* (jealousy), *ta'avah* (temptation), and *kavod* (honor), and our habits are far from perfect, but generally speaking, we're not robbers and thieves. We are therefore in for a double surprise at the tail-end of Yom Kippur. In the *Ne'ilah* service, when we're finally ready to take the plunge and do *teshuvah*, last minute as it is, not only is the longer *Vidui* – confession – of the earlier Yom Kippur prayer missing, but the focus of the *tefillah* seems to accentuate our preoccupation with stealing. I don't understand it! I've finally found the courage to dig down deeply enough into the trenches to create an opening for *teshuvah* – repentance – and I can't even say the *Al Cheit* confession? How will I ever do *teshuvah*? And that phrase that is repeated a number of times – "*l'ma'an nechedal me'oshek yadeinu* – help us put an end to the thievery in our hands." What is all this talk about stealing? I may be a lot of things, but I'm not a thief!

Chazal tell us that Adam Harishon, the first man, was created on Rosh Hashanah (the world was created on the twenty-fifth of Elul) and he was brought to judgment on Rosh Hashanah. His trial was exercised through the verbalization of one word: "*Ayekah* – Where are you?" What happened to you? Why, just a few moments ago you were "*misof ha'olam v'ad sofo* – [you extended] from one end of the earth to the other!" You were "*min ha'aretz v'ad larakia* – [you stretched] from the earth to the heavens." You were so big and so tall; so great and so distinguished! (The name "Adam" shares the same letters as the adverb "*me'od*," which means much, or very.) You were expandable, stretchable, and indefatigable. Even the sky wasn't the limit. *Ayekah*? What has become of that vast potential?

And it is this very question that we need to ask ourselves throughout the Days of Awe. What happened to us? Have we lost our perspective? Have we forgotten who we are? Have we lost sight of the secret of our greatness, that we were created in the image of Hashem? Have we, too, succumbed to the soulless despair of a bankrupt society devoid of all spirituality? Have we become common crooks by stealing a *neshamah* filled with the capacity for greatness and denying it its inherent potential?

At *Ne'ilah*, as the holiest day ebbs away, time is running out. We have to get to the core of *teshuvah* quickly. There's no time for long confessions. What is the essence? What is the nucleus? What is the focus?

It all boils down to one thing. I have to stop stealing! I have to stop cheating! I have to stop deceiving myself! I have to stop living in a finite, *neshamah*-less dream-world and accept the reality that I am created in Hashem's image. I must recognize that I have been gifted with magnificent inner strength that gives me limitless prospects. The Rebbe Reb Bunim *zt"l* would say regarding *Lo Sonu,* the prohibition of cheating one's fellow man, that the way to go *lifnim mishuras hadin* – beyond the letter of the law is to avoid cheating oneself!

Ribono Shel Olam, I beseech You, help me stop cheating myself. Help me stop stealing from the *kochos,* the potential that You implanted within me. Allow me to return to my true being, and in doing so, I will have returned to You, Hashem.

The destruction of the Beis Hamikdash is marked by the reading of *Eichah* (*Lamentations*) on Tishah B'Av. The letters that spell the word "*Eichah*" are the same letters that spell the demand that Hashem made of Adam Harishon when He asked him, "*Ayekah* – What has become of you?" The loss of the Beis Hamikdash is a loss of our perspective of the true dimensions of a man and his ability to build himself as an abode for the *Shechinah's* manifestation. Let us resolve to return to our essence and to do real *teshuvah*. Let us rebuild that Beis Hamikdash within, and surely we will merit the ultimate Beis Hamikdash speedily in our time.

Sukkos – It's Time to Go Home

A mother camel was speaking to her baby camel when her baby asked her, "Mom, why do I have these huge, three-toed feet?"

"Well, son, when we trek across the desert, your large toes will help you stay on top of the soft sand," said his mom.

Absorbing his mother's answer, the young camel asked, "Mom, why have I got these unusually long eyelashes?"

"They are to keep the sand out of your eyes during those dreadful sandstorms on our long trips through the desert," his mother answered.

"Mom, why do I have these giant humps on my back?" the curious baby camel continued to inquire.

"We are blessed with those humps to allow us to store great quantities of water, so we can go without drinking for long periods of time during our journeys across the arid expanse of the desert," his mother responded.

The kid summed it up. "So, we have huge feet to stop us from sinking in the desert sand, long eyelashes to protect our eyes from the sand, and these humps to store water."

"Yes, dear," said his proud mother.

"One more question, Mom," the young camel said. "So why are we living in the San Diego zoo?"

We live in the protection of the shelter of our homes. Our home offers us a roof over our heads, which guarantees our safety and refuge. Our home warms us from the cold and cools us from the heat. It is our pride and our joy, as the saying goes: "A man's home is his castle." Our home is our address, our identity, and it is filled with coziness and nostalgia. It makes us feel snug and secure. It is our trustworthy asylum. But it's still not our home.

Once a year, we exit our homes, referred to as our *diras keva* – permanent abode – and enter our sukkah, our *diras ara'i* – temporary abode – for seven (or eight) days of celebration. We leave the security of our well-constructed dwellings to live under the shade and protection of the trusted One Above. After weeks of *teshuvah* and spiritual cleansing, which has led us to the unequivocal conclusion of *"ein od milvado* – there is no one else besides Him," we demonstrate our absolute *bitachon* in our rejuvenated conviction, and abandon the facade of our earthly domicile in favor of residing in the welcoming arms of the *Eibishter*. We are like the child cradled in the arms of his mother, traversing from safer neighborhoods to more dangerous ones. Regardless of the risk, the child knows only the warmth and protection of his mother's embrace. With this innocence and unflinching trust and faith in the Oneness of our Creator, we joyously enter the sukkah.

The sublime joy a Jew feels in this revived relationship with the *Eibishter* is what distinguishes the Yom Tov of Sukkos as "*Zman Simchaseinu*". There is no joy that compares to the unraveling of doubts, and through the purifying process of the preceding weeks, all dubiety has been replaced with the unambiguous truth of "*Hashem is G-d, in the heavens above and in the earth below; there is none other.*" (Devarim 4:35) Now we can readily understand the Kotzker Rebbe's *vort* with regard to the halachah that someone who is uncomfortable is exempt from sitting in the sukkah. Although the words are conventionally understood as a halachic exemption, the Kotzker Rebbe *zt"l* explains it as a declaration of fact: If inclement weather or the like can interfere with the sublime joy a Jew should feel in communing with the *Ribono Shel Olam* in His abode, to the point that it makes him uncomfortable, indeed, he is exempt from the mitzvah of sukkah, for he has no connection to the lofty opportunity before him.

The Gemara (*Avodah Zarah* 2) speaks about the complaint that the nations of the world will have in the future: "Had You lifted the mountain over our heads and forced us to accept the Torah, as You did to the Jews, perhaps we also would have responded in the affirmative!" Hashem's response will be to give them another chance, and of all the *mitzvos* He'll direct them to fulfill the mitzvah of sukkah. Their willpower will then be tested by the unusual heat of the sun, and in disgust they will defiantly leave the unbearably hot sukkah, kicking it as they exit and thus relinquishing an opportunity for eternity.

The Gemara asks: Why will they be blamed when one who is uncomfortable is exempt from the mitzvah of sukkah? A Jew under the identical circumstances would also be exempt! The answer the Gemara gives is that, granted, one is exempt from remaining in the sukkah under such circumstances, but does one kick it as he exits? Notwithstanding the law that one who experiences discomfort is exempt from the sukkah, were one to truly feel that when he enters a sukkah he resides in the shade of the Almighty, he would hardly suffer any discomfort. In fact, his real discomfort would be that he is being forced to leave the intimacy he enjoys with his Creator. The very fact that the nations' discomfort could elicit such a loathsome response, rather than to humbly leave the sukkah, negates their claim that they truly wish to serve Hashem.

Dovid Hamelech asks Hashem to grant him the privilege of living in the House of G-d his entire life ("*shivti b'veis Hashem kol yemei chayai*"), yet at the end of the *passuk* he asks that he merely merit to visit there ("*u'levakker b'heichalo*"). Many suggest that Dovid Hamelech was asking that he merit to dwell in the House of Hashem permanently, with the same enthusiasm and longing as one who simply visits from time to time. Most of us are not *zocheh* to live in the House of Hashem in a permanent way, but at the very least, once a year, when we are enjoined to enter the sukkah in our yearly visit to the House of Hashem, we should do so with the eagerness and pining of one who merely has the opportunity to be a visitor there. Then we will have tasted what it truly means to go home.

Chanukah – Instant Kedushah

A man ran to the twenty-four-hour convenience store at two in the morning, only to find the owner closing up for the night.

"What are you doing?" the man protested. "You can't be closing! Your sign says: 'Open Twenty-Four Hours!'"

"Yeah," the owner replied. "But not in a row!"

We live in a world where everything is at our fingertips twenty-four hours a day, seven days a week, without interruption. One can shop to his heart's delight from the convenience of his home, at any time of the day or night, as long as he's online and has that indispensable piece of plastic, a credit card. Cars can be started and warmed up from the comfort of one's home; trunks pop open and car doors are unlocked with the push of a button on a key chain. Even the car radio can be adjusted from a control located on the steering wheel, obviating the need to go through the effort of extending one's hand. The GPS precludes any need for asking directions (another *chessed* opportunity lost), as we cruise-control our way through the E-ZPass express toll at sixty miles an hour. The infamous TV remote control allows one to turn the TV on and off, change the channel, the station, the color, the contrast, the tone, the sound, and the decibel all from the comfort of one's bed. (As the story goes, a teenager asks his father: "Dad, is it true that when you were young you actually had to get up to change the channel?")

From the fax machine to the microwave, from the "clap your hands" light to the Shabbos lamp, comfort and convenience has become an expected way of life, and, in the process, a mindset as well. We expect and demand everything to be instantaneous, and we quickly lose patience when it is not.

Unfortunately, this attitude affects our spirituality as well. We want instant *kedushah* – holiness. The popularization of such distortions through books like "*Kabbalah for the Layman*," or through the promotion of Jewish mysticism to fill fleeting impulses for spirituality, only exacerbates this twisted notion. Holiness is a gift from Hashem that only comes through tremendous effort on our parts. Only one who is filled with the knowledge of Gemara and halachah can be prepared to begin approaching such esoteric teachings. In the words of the *Mesillas Yesharim* (ch. 26): "[The acquisition of] holiness begins with effort, and ends with endowment [from Heaven]."

Holiness is not something one simply studies. It is a lifetime occupation of serving Hashem, of scrupulous observance, of character improvement, of willpower, of withstanding temptation, of the mastery of *nigleh*, the revealed Torah. Following that, it may be gifted to him with a gracious endowment of *siyata d'Shmaya*. As the Gemara in *Yoma* (39a) says: "A person who sanctifies himself a little bit, [Heaven] sanctifies him a lot."

It seems almost ludicrous to speak about holiness in a world so saturated with all that is impure. In an atmosphere devoid of all restrictions and inundated with such open-mindedness that has to make one wonder if the world's brains have fallen out in the process, it is difficult to imagine any semblance of *kedushah* whatsoever. Yet, *"Yisrael kedoshim heim* – the Jewish people are holy," and no matter the generation, no matter the climate of the environment, they can nonetheless strive for and achieve their goal. Even in this decadent darkness, a Jew, by toiling in Hashem's Torah and diligently keeping the *mitzvos*, can radiate light. And no matter where he finds himself, the Torah can serve as a beacon of light in the darkest of times, for that light is powered by a higher Authority.

Chanukah, the last of the *yamim tovim* until Mashiach comes, infused in Klal Yisrael the formula to bridge the gap until that auspicious moment (*Pachad Yitzchak, Chanukah ma'amar* 3). Through the victory of a few courageous *Yidden* over the arrogance of the audacious Hellenists who dared to penetrate the Holy of Holies, we absorbed their brazenness, and channeled it into an *azus d'kedushah,* a spiritual confidence that allows us to survive even in the face of wantonness and spiritual abandon (*Ne'os Hadesheh*, Vol. 1, p 160). The very fact that we light the Chanukah candles specifically outdoors, directly in the face of the darkness, within ten *tefachim* of the ground, a place devoid of the *Shechinah*, on the left side, which is traditionally associated with *kochos hatumah*, impure forces, is indication enough of this symbolism (*Ne'os Hadesheh*, Vol. 2, p 222).

Armed with the ammunition of a rejuvenated Torah *shebaal peh*[1], we carry the *azus d'kedushah,* the spiritual confidence, with great pride, and are confident that we will persevere in this dark *galus*; that *kedushah* born out of sweat and travail will triumph and light the way until the time when the *Shechinah* will return to its abode, and we will celebrate the completion of the unfinished symphony of "*Ma'oz Tzur*": "*Az egmor*... – Then I shall complete a song of hymn upon the dedication of the *mizbe'ach*."

---

1. While the Greeks were initially successful in causing forgetfulness of Torah, ironically, that evolved into a spirited rejuvenation of Torah learning that retrieved that which was lost (*Pachad Yitzchak, Chanukah ma'amar* 3).

Purim - Everyone Should Enjoy Purim

It has been said in jest, that the reason why four *pesukim* in *Megillas Esther* are read to the sad tune of *Eichah* (*Lamentations*), is so that the Litvishe Jews (the *"Misnagdim"*) should enjoy Purim as well! If so, the question is asked, why don't they read the entire *megillah* to the somber tune of *Eichah*, if that's what makes them happy?

The rejoining answer is: absolutely not! *Tzu fil hollilus* – That would be too much frivolity!

It is indeed unfortunate that Purim, for some, has become a day of buffoonery and clowning in a wild display of irresponsible inebriation. This "Mardi Gras" approach to a day that is the counterpart of Yom Kippur makes such behavior not only distasteful, but displays a pitifully superficial understanding of the holiness of the day. The true *simchah* of Purim, as well as its auspicious opportunity for growth in a short twenty-four-hour period of time, demands that we reassess our outlook of this special day.

The obvious question is: since when is consuming large measures of alcohol a Jewish trait, let alone a mitzvah? Yet *Chazal* say that a person is obligated to become intoxicated on Purim "to the point that he no longer knows the difference between 'Cursed be Haman' and 'Blessed be Mordechai'." Could it be that our Sages are instructing us to simply get "wasted out of our minds" one day a year in a wild and brainless celebration which leaves its victims mopping up floors and cleaning their carpets? A closer examination of the terminology of *Chazal's* words is in order.

In addition to *Chazal's* uncharacteristic directive to imbibe, their expression of "*l'vesumei b'Purya*," which literally means "to sweeten through Purim" (as opposed to "becoming drunk with wine," [Rashi]), as well as their measure of becoming oblivious to the distinction between the despised Haman and the revered Mordechai, begs for interpretation. Would it not have been more correct to write "*l'shikurei b'chamra b'Purya*," that a person is obligated to become intoxicated by drinking wine on Purim, rather than "*l'vesumei b'Purya*," to sweeten through Purim? In addition, isn't it basic "*Hashkafah* 101" for a Jew to clearly recognize the differences between the righteous man and the wicked one at all times and seasons, and never to equate them?

The well-known declaration of *Chazal* of "*Mishenichnas Adar marbim b'simchah* – when Adar is ushered in, we increase in joy" that we sing so gleefully, is actually only part of the quote. The Gemara in *Taanis* (29) says: "*K'sheim she'mishenichnas Av mam'ittin b'simchah, kach mishenichnas Adar marbim b'simchah* – Just as one diminishes his joy with the ushering in of the month of Av, so shall he increase his joy as he ushers in the month of Adar." For some reason, *Chazal* accentuate a correlation between the joy of Adar and the mourning of Av. The use of the words "*k'sheim* – just as" and "*kach* – so too" make this abundantly clear. The reading of the four *pesukim* to the minor diatonic scale of the "*trup*" of *Eichah*, so easily blended into the *megillah* reading by the *baal korei* from the major scale of the "*trup*" of *Esther*, reiterates this curious relationship between mourning and rejoicing. What is this all about?

In the prayer immediately following the *tekiyos* before *Mussaf* on Rosh Hashanah, we say: "*B'shimcha yigilun kol hayom u'b'tzidkascha yarumu* – In Your name, Hashem, they shall rejoice the entire day (and every day), and in Your righteousness they shall exalt You." The *sefarim hakedoshim* point out that, peculiarly, the beginning letters of the words "*b'shimcha yigilun kol hayom*" spell the word "*b'chiyah* – crying". Again, the relationship between rejoicing and mourning is underscored. Apparently, when a Jew focuses on Hashem's Name each and every day, no matter the events of that day, then his crying is on par with his rejoicing. For the cry of a Jew is never the cry of discouragement and despair, but rather one of hope and trust in the Name of Hashem. His tears are inevitably tears of joy, as his closeness with his Creator is enhanced by virtue of his plight.

This enigma is further reconciled by our firm belief that the *Ribono Shel Olam* is indeed entirely good, and His will is only to do good, although at times that good is concealed from us. The halachah of *"k'sheim shem'varchim al hatov, kach mevarchim al hara* – just as we bless [Hashem] for the good, so we must bless [Him] for the bad" is a manifestation of our steadfast conviction that whatever Hashem does is for the good. To the true believer, there is nothing that transpires during the course of his life that is not part of the master-plan of the Master-planner to benefit him in some way.

Even so, it is rare that we are privileged to see the whole picture that unequivocally reveals the unraveling of the mystery and the revelation of Hashem's glory in its wake. Purim is one of those rare occasions. The amazing reversal of events allowed all of Klal Yisrael to witness the good in the guise of bad in full exposure. The halachah of *"k'sheim shem'varchim al hatov, kach mevarchim al hara"* became a simple matter, as Klal Yisrael basked in the glory of having seen the whole picture.

We can well understand why the joy of Adar is part and parcel of the mourning of Av, as that joy is not limited to the appreciation of the good, but heightened by the appreciation of the bad, as well, as part of that symphony. The *"K'sheim she'mishenichnas Av mam'ittin b'simchah, kach mishenichnas Adar marbim b'simchah"* relationship is identical to the *"k'sheim shem'varchim al hatov, kach mevarchim al hara"* relationship of good and bad. It is all good in the whole picture.

Now it all makes sense. It's not the irresponsible drinking of wine that should intoxicate us as much as Purim itself and the revelation of G-d being ever-present in the natural world; that indeed "*yesh Hashem b'kirbeinu* – Hashem is in our midst!"[2] A person is obligated "*l'vesumei*," to sweeten, that is, to find the sweetness in what appears to be a harsh decree, to see the good in the bad[3], "*b'Purya*," through the amazing revelation of Purim, until the point where he recognizes that even the wickedness of Haman is the equivalent of the good of Mordechai in the bigger and broader picture.

It was Erev Rosh Chodesh Adar 5768 toward evening, as the new month of Adar Sheini was about to begin. A dear friend and I were on our way to Har Nof. We had just made the right turn from Sderot Herzl and were about to pass Yeshivat Merkaz Harav. Then we saw the police, the street roped off, people running frantically, and we heard the screams, and then the shots ring out which mercilessly took the lives of the eight *kedoshim* (*H"yd*). Even after we were whisked away from the scene, we remained frozen in shock from what we had just witnessed.

That night, I was scheduled to speak at Yeshivas Ner Yaakov, at a gathering to celebrate Rosh Chodesh Adar and the feeling of euphoria that it usually generates. But this year was different. We all sat there, stunned by the events of the evening, trying desperately to reconcile how such a feeling of mourning could co-exist with a call to increase in joy. Then it came together. The greatest joy possible is to feel the presence of the *Ribono Shel Olam*, to feel close to Him, to recognize how small we are and how great He is; to understand how desperately we are dependent on

---

2. See *Nesivos Shalom*.

3. בשם רבי ומורי הרב יעקב משה קולפסקי זצ״ל.

Him and how incapable we are without His constant infusion of life and vitality; to perceive that our knowledge is so limited, and that we therefore subjugate ourselves to His mastery of the world and all that transpires – for Hashem sees and knows the whole picture. With tears in our eyes, we rejoiced in the knowledge that someday we will merit to see the good even in such a calamity, and we will recognize deeply in our hearts that *"Hashem is the G-d in the heavens above and in the earth below; there is none other."* (Devarim 4:39)

Pesach – Freedom of Religion

The Israeli couple has been in line at the bank for over two hours. Oded has no more patience for all of the bureaucracy and announces to his wife, "I can't take this any longer! I've had enough of this! I'm going to the Knesset to kill the Prime Minister!" With that, he storms out of the building.

An hour later he returns to the bank. His wife is still in line.

"Where did you go? You ran out of here like a crazy man," she scolds.

"I really went to the Knesset to kill the Prime Minister. I couldn't take it anymore."

"Nu!" says his wife. "So why didn't you kill him?"

"Are you kidding?" Oded responds. "You should see the line over there!"

We tend to think the grass is greener on the other side of the fence. We make the tragic error of defining our terms by the secular world's definitions, thinking they have something that we don't. Our pursuit of freedom and opportunity has succumbed to this pattern as well. How many times have we opted to explore their ways, to taste their freedom, rather than to direct our attention to the clear-cut definition of *Chazal*?

It is *Chazal* who stated it unequivocally: "*Ein lecha ben chorin ela mi she'oseik b'talmud Torah* – The only free man is the one who is immersed and involved in the study of Torah [and the performance of its *mitzvos*]."

Chazal are not telling us that involvement in Torah is one of the many aspects of freedom, but rather "*ein lecha*" – there is *no other* definition of freedom except for this. The source for this is the Torah's description of the *luchos* – the two Tablets of stone – as "*charus* – engraved" with the words of the *Aseres Hadibros*. *Chazal* comment: Don't read the word as "*charus* – engraved," but rather, as "*cheirus* – freedom". The Torah is emphasizing that the essence of those *luchos*, the Torah as given at Har Sinai, is that much-coveted freedom that we seek. In toiling in the Torah , we will realize our objective to truly be free.

How many songs have been sung about freedom here in the Land of the Free? From "*Born Free*" to "*Freedom's Just Another Word for Nothing Left to Lose*," the beats may be catchy, but the lyrics are destructive. We are born to toil in Torah, and in that we achieve freedom. We recognize unequivocally that true freedom is much more than just a word; it's another world and dimension, through which there is everything to gain, both in this world and the next. How well they have taught us that freedom means to do what you want, when you want, with whom you want, wherever you want, in front of the entire world if you want, and then you will never "want," for it will all be yours! Nothing could be further from the truth.

Growing up in America, we develop many loves and interests. They rapidly become part of us, making detachment from them quite difficult, if not downright impossible. We are quickly enslaved. With all of our "choices" and "freedoms," we become swiftly entrapped and ensnared, even to the point of addiction. Without structure or discipline, and more importantly, without the inspiration to free ourselves from the shackles of our earthly pulls, we are doomed to live our lives as others would dictate. This includes dressing like them, speaking like them, being – unfortunately – "free" like them.

Our perspective is quite different. Dovid Hamelech wrote in *Tehillim* (116:16): "*I beseech You, Hashem, for I am Your servant; I am Your servant, the son of Your handmaiden. You have released (freed) me from my bondage.*" How can one be at the same time both a servant and free? How can these two concepts co-exist?

The resolution to this seeming contradiction serves as the very basis of our perception of Torah-true freedom.

The *Ribono Shel Olam* gave us a Torah that allows us to escape what might otherwise enslave us, as it says, "I created the *yetzer hara*, and I created the Torah as an antidote." The aristocracy of Klal Yisrael has always been the noble *talmid chacham* – the one who is a master of serving his own Master, the servant of Hashem who is privileged to work on himself until he can imitate the very *middos* of his Creator .

He is the personification of *Chazal's* definition of a strong person – someone who conquers his *yetzer* through toiling in Torah, which enables him to use all of his strengths and capabilities to serve Hashem. Indeed he is free, free to be the master over his *middos*; free to be the master over his tongue; free to escape the powerful and unyielding clutches of jealousy and desire, which can utterly control and ultimately destroy a person. Instead, he allows his soul to influence his baser instincts, in order to produce this majestic member of the Jewish people.

For the Jew who recognizes that actualizing his full spiritual potential is his *raison d'etre*, and the structure and discipline of the Torah is the means to accomplish that goal, there is no contradiction whatsoever in the words of Dovid Hamelech. It is specifically *because* "I am your servant," and I humble myself to Your Torah, that I am "released from my bondage." This is my greatest privilege and thrill!

When we absorb the teachings of *Chazal* and work on refining our *middos*, that's when we are free. When we are able to control our mouths from utterances of *lashon hara* and *rechilus*, that's when we are free. When we overpower our evil inclinations, when we give up the many desires of our hearts for objectives of much greater importance, that's when we are free. When we can finally prioritize our lives and decide, once and for all, what is important and what is not, what is eternal and what is only a poor substitute, what is essential and what is excess, what will nurture our *neshamah* and allow us to actualize its great potential and what will lead us in the opposite direction, that's when we can truly be free.

Then we can escape the "*matzar*" – the inescapable constraints of Mitzrayim, and merit the epitome of freedom; the freedom to have elevated our *guf* to serve its *neshamah* counterpart, as together they unite in the pursuit of closeness to Hashem. And only then will we be free to return our *neshamah* to its Creator, free to bask in the Divine Presence of the Almighty Himself for eternity.

Shavuos – Wheelbarrows

In Communist Russia, it was not uncommon to rotate factory jobs every thirty days to ensure that no one worker rose to any position of prominence.

Every day in the factory, at 5:00 P.M., one particular comrade would be stopped by the suspicious guard as he approached the exit with his wheelbarrow.

"What exactly are you trying to steal?" the guard would question as he uncovered the wheelbarrow, only to find it empty each time.

This continued for the entire month, and each time it was searched, the wheelbarrow was empty. After the month was up, when jobs were rotated, the two men met at the local pub.

"Comrade," said the former guard, "I know you were stealing something. I am no longer in my former position, so you need not fear me. Tell me, my friend, what exactly were you stealing?"

"It's very simple, comrade," the other man said. "I was stealing wheelbarrows!"

It's so easy to focus on the insignificant and ignore that which is primary. The *ikkar* – main thing is the vessel itself. What type of vessel one is will determine his absorbing potential. To accept the Torah properly, one needs to prepare himself beforehand, in order to maximize the depth and security of that reception. It's easy to "run without the ball" and fumble away the opportunity of a lifetime that every Yom Tov of Shavuos offers us, the opportunity to once again accept the Torah. Jews don't simply celebrate a Yom Tov as a ceremonious commemoration of past events; rather, they revisit and relive that event and thereby enjoy the opportunities that its holiness and sparks affords them. As Shavuos approaches, we need to prepare ourselves to be that special vessel for an actual new *Kabbalas HaTorah*.

And what is that vessel like? It is simple and humble. It resembles the desert in which the Torah was given. It mimics the mountain that was chosen for the giving of the Torah – the lowest of them all. It fashions itself after the man who was entrusted to transmit that Torah to the Jewish People – Moshe Rabbeinu, the most humble of mankind. It is inspired by a Klal Yisrael who, like angels, realize that their entire existence is inextricably contingent on their one mission of fulfilling the will of Hashem, and therefore humbly accepts that mission without question, proclaiming "*na'aseh* – we will do" before "*nishma* – we will hear."

One of the reasons given for the custom to eat dairy on Shavuos is linked to the above. Milk and milk products, when stored in fancy vessels of silver or gold will spoil rapidly. They need to be in "*pashute keilim*" (simple vessels) of plastic or cardboard. The simple vessel enhances the reception of the milk in the most significant manner, as it preserves its content.

Some of the most noble and refined Jews are "*pashute Yidden*" (simple Jews) whose *emunah peshutah* – simple faith and absolute adherence to making Hashem's will be their own will, make them sublime vessels, and their *Kabbalas HaTorah* one to admire. Let us be resolute to make ourselves into worthy, simple vessels, so that the *Shechinah* will rest within us, and the holy Torah will radiate from us with a glow of brilliance and splendor for all to behold.

Tishah B'av-Tears Of Hope: Turn A Tear Into A Prayer

A dear friend of mine, a prominent *rav*, was going through a difficult illness. A person of refined character, he tried hard to remain upbeat and optimistic for the sake of his wife and children. He was therefore quite surprised when one morning the nurse walked into his room and scolded: "Rabbi, be positive!"

The rabbi was taken aback by the nurse's comment, given that he was working so hard on maintaining a smiling face of good cheer, in the midst of experiencing his own personal emotional roller-coaster. When she returned to his room at the end of her shift, he was unable to hold back his tears as he questioned her reproach.

"I've tried so hard to keep my chin up and weather the storm. I thought I was doing a pretty good job, until your comment this morning. Am I doing something wrong?"

"No! No! Rabbi, not at all! Yesterday, you asked me what your blood-type was. I was just giving you the test results. It's B positive!"

Rav Yaakov Yosef Herman (subject of the biography *All for the Boss*) was a maverick in his zealousness to uphold authentic *Yiddishkeit,* in an American community that, for the most part, didn't care. At his daughter's wedding, he innovated that there be separate dancing for men and women, that the women dress in modest attire and that *benchers* be distributed to all the tables. In addition, he paid the caterer for dessert, but instructed that it not be served, *zeicher l'churban* – to tone down the celebration in memory of the *Beis Hamikdash*. He was from a rare breed of Jews, who deeply felt the lack of a *Beis Hamikdash*.

The Ribnitzer Rebbe *zt"l* would dress in sackcloth the entire Tishah B'Av, as he lamented the destruction of the *Beis Hamikdash* and all the calamities that have befallen Klal Yisrael throughout the generations. In his great sensitivity to what the *Beis Hamikdash* represented, he was able to relive the tragedy, the tears flowing naturally from his holy eyes.

Unfortunately, for most of us it is difficult to conjure up a tear, even on Tishah B'Av, let alone the rest of the year. I remember as a child trying to survive Tishah B'Av, rather than observe it. All too often, this survival attitude remains with us into our adult years, and we end up lamenting the length of the *kinnos davening* more than the loss of Hashem's abode.

Not only are we unable to cry, but we are deprived of an important foundation of *Yiddishkeit*: how to cry like a Jew.

The *passuk* (*Shemos* 2:6) describes how *Bas Pharaoh* sees the baby Moshe in a basket in the river: "*And she saw the boy, and behold the youth was crying.*" She then observed, "*He must be from the children of the Hebrews* (although the Egyptian male babies were cast into the river as well)". The *passuk* seems to base her recognition of his origin on the hearing of his crying, prompting the Slonimer Rebbe *zt"l* to ask: Was it possible to discern between the cry of a Jew and the cry of a *goy*?

Indeed there is a distinction. The cry of a Jew is a cry of hope. The cry of *goy* is a cry of despair. The cry of a Jew is a cry for the future. The cry of a *goy* is one of hopelessness. Our tears are tears of sadness, but at the same time they are tears of faith in the *Ribono Shel Olam's chessed* and impending *yeshuah* – salvation. Ours are heartfelt tears, bewailing all the devastation of being exiled from Yerushalayim (*betzeisi meYerushalayim*), but they look ahead to the song of ecstasy of when we will return to Yerushalayim. "Gladness and joy (will prevail) while anguish and sighing will flee, when I return to Jerusalem (*Beshuvi leYerushalayim*)." *(Kinnos L'Tishah B'Av)* This is our signet, our legacy, the expertise and the craft (*umnus*) of our ancestors. Our slogan has always been what Chizkiyahu Hamelech taught us *(Brachos 10b)*: "*Afilu cherev chada* – Even if a sharp sword is pointed at one's neck, he should not refrain from imploring for and hoping for Hashem's mercy." No matter what the situation is, our motto is: "be positive."

For this reason, the *keruvim* (the angelic figures attached to the Holy Ark) were embracing one another during the actual *churban (Yoma 54b)*, even though they typically would display estrangement when Klal Yisrael incurred Hashem's wrath. For this reason, too, there is no *tachanun* on Tishah B'Av, for the *passuk* promises *(Eichah 1:15)* "*Kara alai mo'ed,*" one day it will become a *mo'ed* (a festival). Although that day has not yet come, the anticipation of good times is already present in our tears. In a way, the homelessness, so to speak, of *Hakadosh Baruch Hu* results in His living among us, which makes Him even more accessible. This idea is hinted to in the *passuk* in *Eichah* (1:3), "*Kol rodfeha hisiguha bein hametzarim,*" all who pursue Hashem can access him during the three weeks known as Bein Hametzarim. For this reason, tradition tells us that the *Mashiach* will be born on Tishah B'Av. Rather than standing in contradiction to the essence of the day, it is part and parcel of the positive aspects of the crying of a Jew.

Let us understand that the root of Tishah B'Av's designation as a day of tragedy for all generations (the expulsion of the Jews from Spain; World War I, which had great implications for the Holocaust that took place in the second world war, broke out on Tishah B'Av; even the destruction of the twin towers on 9/11 has a hint of Tishah B'Av – the 9th day of the 11th month-Av) was the *cheit* of the *Meraglim* – the spies who were sent ahead while the Jews waited in the desert to hear about Eretz Yisrael. They returned with their negative report about Eretz Yisrael, and Klal Yisrael cried. Hashem rebuked them, "You cried for no reason. I will give you reason to cry for all future generations." Tishah B'Av was established as the day of calamity for all future generations because of a negative report, and an unwarranted cry. It was the cry of a *goy* and not the cry of a Yid. It was full of hopelessness – a cry filled with negativity. It didn't include the *Ribono Shel Olam*. And therefore, the *tikkun* – rectification – for that demands a cry accompanied by hope and promise; one of rebuilding and repairing; a cry that that yearns for closeness to Hashem.

The *passuk* in Tehillim says "*B'shimcha yegilun kol hayom* – In your name do we rejoice all day." The first letters of each word spell out the word *b'chiyah*, the Hebrew word for crying. What does crying have to do with rejoicing? For a Yid there is everything connecting the two. When a Jew cries like a Jew, he rejoices in the impending salvation. He rejoices in his never-ending relationship with his Father in Heaven. In Your name do we rejoice "*kol hayom* – the entire day" not only the entire day, but every day; even the most tragic; even the worst imaginable, even on Tishah B'Av; and especially on Tishah B'Av.

There was a young boy, whose father had to discipline him, and the young boy began to cry. Almost immediately, he took a *siddur* and began to *daven*. Upon being asked by his father to explain his unusual behavior, he said, "If I'm already crying, I might as well put the tears to good use." (Tears are one of the most powerful mediums of *tefillah*.) This young, positive thinker turned out to be one of the *gedolei hador*, Harav Baruch Ber Leibovitz *zt"l*.

Our task is to turn every tear into a prayer. Whether we are peeling onions, or preparing the *maror* on Erev Pesach, or *chas v'shalom* bemoaning a serious life issue, let us always remember how precious the tears of *Yidden* are to Hashem when they are used as a conduit to bring us closer to Him. *Bas*

Pharaoh heard the cry of the child and was able to discern the hopefulness in his voice that convinced her that it was a Jewish child. Let us make sure that our tears include the positive energy of "*Hayipalei meHashem davar* – Is anything impossible for G-d?" (*Bereishis* 18:14) And the *Ribono Shel Olam* will respond in kind, as we sing and dance upon our return to Yerushalayim.

Internal Struggles

Compartmentalization: Light and Darkness All In One

The two women stood before the *rav*, each one confident that her claim was valid. It seemed that the same young man had been suggested as a *shidduch* for both of their daughters. Each mother now claimed that he had been offered to her first, and therefore, her daughter reserved the right to marry this boy. After they'd presented their claims, the *rav* came to a decision:

"Being that neither of you can prove which of you was initially contacted regarding this *shidduch*, I have no recourse but to slice him in half, so that you can share him. Bring the sword!"

"No! No!" screamed out one of the mothers. "I can't allow a Jew to die on my account!"

"Kill him!" said the other mother. "It's the only fair thing to do!"

"Ah!" said the *rav*, addressing the second mother. "The *shidduch* is yours! You must be the real mother-in-law!"

Could a person simultaneously broker a marriage and condone the cold-blooded murder of the groom? Absolutely! There are well-dressed, sophisticated people who could murder in a suit and tie, careful not to become soiled with their victim's blood, because they are on their way to their kid's PTA meeting. There are Senators and Congressmen, politicians of all stripes, servants of the people, graduates of the most prestigious universities, who will espouse any policy that will help further their career, regardless of how that course of action will endanger their fellow countrymen. There are journalists and members of the media who, contrary to the very creed of their professions, will report the news with absolute bias, to the detriment and jeopardy of their own armed forces and defenders of their very nation. There are members of the clergy who have dedicated their lives to teaching their constituency morality and ethics, who are guilty of the worse indiscretions and licentiousness. How can intelligent people conduct their lives in such total contradiction?

Everyone is familiar with the story of the two women who came before Shlomo Hamelech with a baby that both claimed to be hers. Rav Chaim Shmulevitz *zt"l* writes: Consider the psyche of the woman who stole the other's child and was willing to have the child put to death rather than to surrender it to its real mother. At first glance, she seems to be the lowest of the low, cold-hearted, and frigid. On the other hand, note the pining and yearning this woman must have possessed, to give from her natural wellspring of motherly love and self-sacrifice for the sake of a child, to the point that she was willing to stoop so low in order to fulfill her calling. What kind of pathetic monster is this? A Dr. Jekyll and Mr. Hyde mentality! Can there be anything more brutally cruel than to steal another's infant, yet can there be anything more admirable than the *mesiras nefesh* of a mother for her child? Can such diametrically opposed behaviors co-exist in one organism?

Yeravam ben Nevat, the quintessential "*choteh u'machati es harabim* – one who sins and causes others to sin," is a prime example of such conspicuous duality. As he audaciously stood in front of the *navi* sent to rebuke him, fully prepared to sacrifice on his forbidden altar to his idolatry, he displayed behavior so twofaced, that it is mind-boggling.

"And Yeravam sent forth his hand from the altar, commanding, 'Arrest him [the *navi*]!'" The man of G-d had foretold how the priests who sacrificed on such altars to their idolatry would be slaughtered on those very altars by the future king of Yehuda. To make his point unequivocally clear, he declared, as a sign, that the altar upon which Yeravam was about to offer his sacrifice would split in half and its ashes would spill to the ground. King Yeravam, obviously displeased, wanted the *navi* telling him this to be removed from his sight. However, as soon as he extended his hand in the direction of the *Ish HaElokim* (man of G-d), his hand became paralyzed, fixed in position, and he was unable to return it as before. Precisely at that moment, the altar split apart, as predicted, and the ashes poured out to the ground.

One might expect Yeravam to be humbled and enlightened at that auspicious moment, but the darkness that had become the creed of his existence interfered. "And the king responded and he said to the man of G-d, 'Please beseech Hashem, YOUR G-d, and pray for my sake so that my hand shall return to me.' And the man of G-d prayed to Hashem, and the king's hand returned to him as before." How incredible! With absolute recognition that the *Ribono Shel Olam* is the One source of his cure, Yeravam nonetheless brazenly begged, "Pray to your G-d" – and not his!

"And it was as before" – Rashi in *Mishlei* comments that nothing changed! The use of his hand restored, Yeravam continued to serve his idolatry in an amazing display of contradiction, of light and darkness mixed together, completely invulnerable to the obvious truth.

We all know people who can simultaneously utter two conflicting statements out of the same side of their mouths. We probably never considered ourselves to be such people, but no doubt, in our thought process, we are all guilty of such dichotomy. After all, we are only human, and this is part of our essence. The battle of light versus darkness in the heart and mind of mankind has been a historical struggle from time memorial.

We must understand that darkness is not simply the absence of light, but a creation in and of itself, as it says in the blessings of *Krias Shema*, "He creates the light and creates the darkness." Because of this, one could theoretically act like an angel, in a most enlightened fashion, and yet at times exhibit the most degenerative behavior, entrenched in the darkness of this world. Light and darkness are mutually exclusive and do not operate with one being contingent on the other. One must struggle to build fortresses of light, and at the same time uproot and remove the darkness; it is not an automatic process. It is therefore possible, and more likely probable, for one to be filled with light, yet simultaneously sullied by darkness.

Even Torah-observant Jews are susceptible to living a life that is full of contradictions. The balancing act necessary for living a Torah life is difficult, and requires great sagaciousness. In the realm of Torah itself, which has an essence of complete light, darkness can nonetheless penetrate, pervade, and even prevail. And the few authentic, G-d-fearing, *ehrliche Yidden* are left to pick up the pieces of the thousands of casualties of all the subcultures and all the "isms" that not only barely resemble our holy Torah, but are replete with darkness and gross distortion.

The beginning of the solving of any problem is contingent on a keen awareness and identification of the problem. Having identified the reality of the co-existence of light and darkness in the human psyche, we need to attack on two fronts with the hope that a little bit of light diffuses a lot of darkness. And each time we rise to the challenge and choose good over bad, each time we overcome and overpower the potential darkness within, we reveal a beacon of light that will illuminate the path to eternity.

Enemies in the West

The knight was reporting on the war effort to the king.

"Your Majesty, we have vanquished your adversaries in the south; we have removed the menace from the east; we have annihilated the opposition in the north; and we have demolished your enemies in the west."

"Enemies in the west?" asked the king. "I don't have any enemies in the west!"

"Well," replied the knight, "now you do!"

We are forever grateful for the freedom we enjoy in the "west" that allows us to observe our religious practices without concern of persecution. To be sure, we would be naive to think that we are free of enemies. Anti-Semitism is on the rise in Western culture. Even in some democracies, Jews can no longer walk the streets wearing yarmulkas on their heads, for fear of attack.

Our greatest enemy in the West, however, is the very freedom that we enjoy. It is this freedom that has contributed to a spiritual Holocaust of catastrophic proportions. With all due respect to the awe-inspiring *Teshuvah* Movement, assimilation continues to spiral out of control. Whereas in the past, Jews were scorned in certain typical gentile settings, today, in the spirit of "tolerance" and "political correctness," they are enthusiastically welcomed, and unfortunately fall prey to integration.

Prophetically, Yaakov Avinu warns us to beware of Eisav when he acts like our "brother," as indicated in his prayer: "*Save me from the hands of my brother, from the hands of Eisav.*" (*Bereishis* 32:12) What appears to be a redundancy (after all, we know Yaakov's only brother is Eisav), serves as a forewarning that when Eisav acts like our brother and invites us into his life, he is even a more grievous foe than when he acts like the wicked "Eisav".

Today, we are bombarded with shells of visual ammunition that pull us into a world where the *yetzer hara* has free reign. And even when that attack is not fully invasive in the physical realm, nonetheless, our minds and our hearts are overwhelmingly exposed, at the very least, to a vicarious secular existence, powered by a formidable foe. What are we to do?

Chazal tell us: "*Barasi yetzer hara u'barasi lo Torah tavlin* – I've created the evil inclination, and I've created the Torah as a remedy for it." In the spirit of the principle, "The cure always preceeds the infliction," Hashem advanced the creation of the Torah two thousand years before the creation of man, *yetzer hara* included. Although typically understood in this light, the choice of the word "*tavlin*" to mean "remedy," as opposed to the more commonly used word, "*refuah*," is puzzling. After all, "*tavlin*" does not really mean "remedy" – it means spice!

A spice enhances the taste of food which otherwise would be bland, and brings out its flavor to ensure its good taste. Chazal are revealing to us a great secret: Torah does not "remedy." It channels. It directs the inexorable and unrelenting power of that *yetzer hara*, and appropriates it for good use. Indeed, it heightens a force that otherwise would lead to negativity, and instead, produces from it a vitality and vibrancy, a surge of positive energy that allows a *ben aliyah* to overcome and overpower all obstacles, to stretch and expand in a way that seems not humanly possible.

Consider the following: One of the greatest compliments is to be deemed a *baal chessed* – one who consistently engages in kind deeds. Yet, the very same word, *chessed*, is also used in the *passuk* to describe the shameful act of an illicit incestuous relationship between a brother and sister. The *passuk* says: "*A man who shall take his sister, the daughter of his father or the daughter of his mother, and he sees her nakedness, and she shall see his nakedness, it is a disgrace ("chessed hu"), and they shall be cut off before their people...*" (*Vayikra* 20:17) How could the same word that stands for benevolence and sensitivity, also connote disgrace and shame of the most promiscuous nature, for which the parties involved are liable for excision?

A possible explanation underscores the significance of channelization in *avodas* Hashem. The passion within a person can be utilized for good, as kindness and generosity, or for bad, manifesting itself in such extreme licentiousness. *Chessed* is that passion; that force. When directed properly, one can maximize its energy to achieve the loftiest levels of piety; when misdirected, it can become one's ruination.

Our ability to channel this *ko'ach hayetzer* comes to us honestly. It is an inheritance from our ancestors. When Yaakov Avinu defeated the angel of Eisav in their wrestling match, he was empowered over the "forces of evil." His name was changed to Yisrael. Eisav, the quintessential symbol of the *yetzer hara*, the Satan, is now in Yaakov's domain to be utilized for the good. The numerical value of "Yisrael," which is 541, is equivalent to the combination of "Yaakov" (182) and "Satan" (359). Yisrael lives up to his name when he overwhelms the Satan and channels that great force to his own spiritual advantage.

"Yisrael" is also an acronym for "*yesh shishim ribo osios laTorah* – there are 600,000 letters in the Torah." These 600,000 letters correspond to the 600,000 members of Klal Yisrael. Every Jew has his own portion in the Torah, and it is through the personification of his unique portion that he absorbs the "*tavlin*" that will empower him over all forces within, to serve his Creator with all of his heart.

Here Today, Gone Tomorrow

Abe and Murray, two elderly Jewish men, are strolling down the street one day when they happened to pass a church. Outside on the lawn, a large sign is posted that reads: "Convert and Receive $100 – FREE!"

Abe stops for a moment and stares at the sign.

"Abe! What's going on?" asks Murray. "You're not serious, are you?"

"Yeah! I'm serious!" Abe replies. "I sure could use a hundred dollars! I'm going in!" With that, Abe strides purposefully into the church. He exits twenty minutes later with his head bowed.

"So!" says Murray. "Did you get the hundred dollars?"

Abe looks up at him and says, "Is that all you people ever think about?"

―※―

Generally, a person does not transform from one level of observance to the opposite extreme so swiftly. Such a rapid metamorphosis goes against the laws of nature of the evil inclination. The power of the *yetzer hara* is to work little by little. "So is the craft of the *yetzer hara*: Today, he tells him [the person], 'Do this.' Tomorrow, he tells him, 'Do that.' – Until he tells him, 'Go serve idolatry.' " (*Shabbos* 105) A little bit today, a bit more tomorrow. Although initially the *yetzer hara's* ultimate goal may be extremely far away, a fast transfiguration seems beyond its strength.

Yet, at times we find that individuals, or even Klal Yisrael as a whole, descended from the highest level of observance to heresy and apostasy in record time. A case in point is the sin of the Golden Calf. That a generation that was witness to the splitting of the sea and all the miracles in Mitzrayim; that a *Dor De'ah*, standing at Har Sinai and pointing with their finger at the revelation of the *Shechinah* while saying, "*Zeh Keili v'anveihu* – This is my G-d and I will glorify Him," could suddenly worship a molten image cast from gold, is an enigma that requires explanation. This is especially true when one considers the limited ability of the *yetzer hara* to achieve such a dramatic reversal. The *passuk* itself underscores this very point when it writes: "*They turned away so quickly from the path that I commanded them and made for themselves a golden calf.*" (*Shemos* 32:8) How could it have happened so quickly?

It wasn't so simple. Klal Yisrael was tricked by the Satan. On that fateful day, he showed them a mirage: the image of the coffin of Moshe, their great leader. The sky blackened; darkness enveloped them. A climate of gloom and doom, disappointment and despondency surrounded them. Their leader was gone, and an overwhelming fear overcame them.

With a nation gripped by panic and despair in his hands, the stage was set for the Satan to go in for the kill. No longer limited by his typical power of small incremental gains, but rather empowered exponentially by virtue of Klal Yisrael's depression, he was prepared for a windfall profit. Such is the strength of the Satan when we are down, explains Rav Chaim Shmulevitz zt"l in his classic *sefer*, *Sichos Mussar*. Even a *Dor De'ah* can be transformed into a nation of idol-worshipers.

It had been Kayin – not Hevel – who had conceived the idea to bring a sacrifice to Hashem (see Ramban). The notorious Kayin was actually the first to comprehend the secret of sacrificial offerings. He clearly was an *oved* Hashem. Yet, when Hashem did not respond to his more frugal offering, as He did to his brother Hevel's more generous one, Kayin lapsed into a fit of anger and envy that led to his infamous act of murder. Targum Yonasan adds a new dimension: In a moment's time, Kayin went from being an *oved* Hashem to a *kofer b'ikar* (heretic). In his rage and fury at Hashem's rejection of his sacrifice, he denied the fundamental concepts of reward and punishment and of the World to Come, and declared blasphemously: "*Leis din v'leis dayan* – There is no judgment and no Judge!"

Again we ask: how could he have fallen so swiftly? Such power is not the domain of the *yetzer hara*! However, when one has "lost it," when he is filled with despair, when he is consumed by such all-controlling, bad character traits as anger and jealousy, his *yetzer* is empowered and anything is possible *r"l*.

We live in a world that is shaky and forever changing. The daily news is shocking and horrifying. The ups and downs of life threaten our security, and it is easy to slip into frustration and despondency. As Jews, we must be cognizant that to do so would increase the power of the Satan to destroy us. It is difficult enough to deal with the unrelenting attack of the *yetzer hara* in its normal, slow, and deliberate fashion. We dare not expedite the process and facilitate the *yetzer hara's* power by allowing ourselves to fall into lapses of anger and depression!

Let us resolve to serve Hashem with *simchah* and remove this menace, little by little, through our meticulous mitzvah observance. Let us be determined to never lend added strength to the enemy.

Who is Like You Hashem?

The *shidduch* seemed to be going well, and Rena's father felt it was time to have a serious talk with Chaim about his future plans. Upon Chaim's arrival, he invited the boy to sit down in the living room, and began his interrogation.

"So, Chaim, can I ask you what your plans are for the future?"

"With Hashem's help, I would like to sit and learn as long as I can," Chaim responded enthusiastically.

"That's wonderful," Rena's father said. "But how do you expect to support yourself down the road?"

"*Der Eibishter* will help," Chaim replied.

"What I mean is, after a few children *im yirtzeh* Hashem, how will you make a living?" Rena's father clarified.

"The *Ribono Shel Olam* will help!" Chaim answered once again.

"How long do you think you can hold out?" Rena's father persisted.

"Hashem will take care of us!" Chaim replied again.

Later that evening, upon returning home from the date, Rena asked her father what he thought about Chaim.

"He's a lovely young man," her father replied. "There's just one problem. He thinks that I'm the *Ribono Shel Olam*!"

Although the Torah instructs us to follow in the ways of Hashem, as it says, "*V'halachta b'drachav* – and you should go in his ways (*Devarim* 28:9)," we certainly can never equal His greatness. We attempt to emulate His *middos* in the spirit of the Gemara in *Shabbos* (133b): "Just as He (G-d) is merciful, you should also be merciful; just as He is benevolent, you should also be benevolent." And yet at the same time, we stand in awe of His goodness, His sensitivity, His patience and forbearance, His uniqueness, His oneness, and so on.

The word for mankind, "*adam*," is related to the word "*adameh* – I will be compared to," for our task in life is to learn as much as we can about our Creator, through studying the Torah and the world around us, and to imitate Him to the best of our ability. Indeed, the Shelah Hakadosh brings the *passuk* in *Yeshayahu* (14:14) as a hint to such aspirations: "*I shall ascend to the high places above the clouds. I shall be likened to the One above.*"

In the classic *sefer Tomer Devorah*, Rav Moshe Cordevero, the Ramak, vividly describes the specifics of the thirteen *middos* of Hashem that we are to simulate and model our lives upon. The *sefer* focuses on verses in *Michah* (7:18-20) that hint at these *middos*.

In describing the first of the thirteen *middos*, "*mi Keil kamocha* – Who is like You, Hashem," the *Ramak* says something powerful enough to shake the most hardened criminal: There is not a moment in the course of one's life that man is not nourished and sustained by virtue of Hashem's benevolence. Even the sinner is included in G-d's graciousness. Thus, no man ever sins against G-d without G-d, at that very moment, bestowing the vitality upon him that allows him the power to move his limbs for sinful purposes. The sinner is being sustained by the king as he slings mud in the king's own face! Hashem grants the sinner life, even as he engages in spiritual suicide. Can there be a more humbling thought?

In a strange way, this rebel stands to gain inspiration in a realm that is exclusive to renegades like him. For it is they who have personally experienced the extent of G-d's greatness and the magnitude of His patience. Perhaps it could be suggested that this is what the Gemara means when it interprets "*V'ahavta es Hashem elokecha b'chol levavcha* – love Hashem with all of your heart(s) (*Devarim* 6:5)," as "with your inclination for bad, the *yetzer hara*, as well as your inclination for good, the *yetzer hatov*." One can readily understand how one serves Hashem with his *yetzer hatov*, but how does one serve Hashem with his *yetzer hara*? The Gemara may be alluding to this very poignant lesson of the *Tomer Devorah*: When one's *yetzer hara* is inflamed, when one is in the heat of the sin, when the evil inclination has gotten the best of him, let him be reminded of Who is sustaining him at that very moment of indiscretion. Serve Hashem with your *yetzer hara* – in those inevitable moments of its success – by invoking the awe-inspiring and humbling idea that *even as I sin, the* Ribono Shel Olam *still sustains me.* This is something that only the sinner can properly appreciate. Serving Hashem with one's *yetzer hara* makes inspiration available to him even at his weakest moments, inspiration that has the power to catapult a sinner from a rebellious servant to an *oveid* Hashem.

There are other ways to serve Hashem through the *yetzer hara*. My father *zt"l*, a person who had a great love for Torah, once told me about an inspirational moment in his life that no doubt contributed to his love for learning. He had the privilege, on a regular basis, to drive his *rebbi,* the eminent Torah giant, Harav Yaakov Yitzchak Halevi Ruderman *zt"l*, to visit the great *gaon* Harav Michoel Forshlager *zt"l*, a close *talmid* of the Avnei Neizer. R' Forshlager lived unobtrusively in downtown Baltimore. My father would describe vividly how the house was furnished from wall to wall and from floor to ceiling with *sefarim*. He related the tremendous respect that Rav Ruderman accorded this great *talmid chacham*. On one occasion, my father took the opportunity to speak with Rav Forshlager, at which time he asked him for advice on how to learn Torah. The great *gaon* responded: "You have to learn Torah with your *yetzer hara!*" My father understood this to mean that one must study Torah with the same unrelenting spirit and determination that the *yetzer hara* demands of us. Indeed, there are many ways to serve Hashem with one's *yetzer*.

The *Ribono Shel Olam*, in His great wisdom, created everything with the potential to be used for the service of Hashem. Even the *yetzer hara* is included. It is obviously preferable to conquer the *yetzer hara*, render it harmless, and serve Hashem with our *yetzer tov*. Nonetheless, the *Ribono Shel Olam* in His eternal kindness provided for us the means to return to Him even from the depths of our failures. Such is the love of our Father in Heaven for His children. There is no one like You, Hashem! But we will try, to the best of our ability, to copy Your every move.

Spiritual Tools

Man's True Strength

A short, scrawny fellow interviewed for a job as a lumberjack. The foreman was unimpressed by his small size, and barely acknowledged him, until the little guy pleaded with the foreman to give him chance.

"Okay, let me see what you can do."

The little guy grabbed an axe and in ten minutes he single-handedly chopped down an entire tree.

"How did you learn to do that?" asked the foreman, wowed by the man's proficiency.

"Oh. I used to chop down trees in the Sahara Forest."

"You mean the Sahara Desert?" asked the foreman.

"Is that what they call it now?"

How enchanted we are with physical prowess! Building muscles has become an obsession. How ironic it is that today's society, which so dramatically worships physical strength, has stripped man of his true strength. It has reduced the stature of man to that of a weakling who is incapable of achieving what the letters of his name, Adam imply: *me'od* – more; growth and expansion (Maharal, *Derech Chaim* 2:1). The original *tzuras ha'adam*, dimension of man, has been replaced by a self-focused, featherweight mindset that stops a person from actualizing his true potential for strength. The Torah view of strength has very little to do with size, and very much to do with *ratzon* – willpower. "*Ein davar ha'omeid bifnei haratzon* – Nothing can stand in the way of willpower."

The original dimensions of Adam, described by *Chazal* (*Sanhedrin* 38b) as "*misof ha'olam ad sofo* – from one end of the world to the other" and "*min ha'aretz ad larakia* – from the earth to the Heavens," amply display how the *tzuras ha'adam*, as intended, was not confined by space. Man stood tall and strong; and although through the sin of Adam Harishon, mankind was diminished (ibid), he nonetheless remained with awesome strength potential. Whether it was the daughter of Pharaoh, who was able to stretch her arm many *amos* to reach the basket that held Moshe Rabbeinu, or Yaakov Avinu, who removed the rock that all of the shepherds could not budge from the top of the well, their strength came from their steadfast belief in the ability of man to expand beyond that which is naturally expected; for nothing can stand in the way of willpower.

R' Chaim Shmulevitz *zt"l* comments (*Sichos Mussar, ma'amar* 32) regarding the apparently miraculous reach of the daughter of Pharaoh, that this was not a double miracle of her arm at first extending beyond its normal reach, and then returning supernaturally to its original size. Indeed, it was not a miracle at all, but rather, she was a *ben adam* – a person who gathered all of her inner strength and reverted back to the *tzuras ha'adam,* the human dimensions of Adam Harishon before he sinned; the Adam Harishon who was "*misof ha'olam ad sofo*" and "*min ha'aretz ad larakia.*"

The *paytan* (poet) in *Tefillas Geshem* defines this phenomenon as *yichud haleiv* – uniting the forces of the heart. He describes the amazing feat of Yaakov Avinu in moving that boulder as "*yichad leiv v'gal even* – he united the forces of his heart and rolled off the rock." The uniting of the forces of one's heart can produce results that transcend nature and surpass all physical expectations and limitations. If the speed of a base runner, attempting to steal second at the bottom of the ninth in the seventh game of the World Series, with two outs and his team down by one run, is enhanced by his tremendous willpower and desire to achieve his goal, how much more so can a person stretch himself for achievement on a spiritual level when *siyata d'Shmaya,* Heavenly assistance, is at his side.

A Jew's spirituality knows no bounds. One look at the words of the *Nefesh Hachaim (sha'ar alef, perek daled)* leaves us staggering at the potential we have. Commenting on the *passuk;* "*T'nu oz l'Elokim* – Give strength to Hashem (*Tehillim* 68:35)," the *Nefesh Hachaim*, obviously puzzled by the idea that a person can give strength to the Almighty, writes: "One should not think, even for a moment, that his lowly deeds are too insignificant to affect anything in the world. Quite the contrary! Every one of his deeds is accounted for according to its *shoresh*, its root, and has its effect in the highest of places." This is so much so, to the point where Hashem, as it were, receives strength from him.

Continuing on this theme, R' Chaim Volozhiner explains the mishnah in *Avos* (2:1), *"Da mah l'ma'alah mimcha."* The mishnah is usually interpreted to mean, "Know that which is above you." R' Chaim suggests that it means that a person should realize that that which is *above*, comes from *within you*. Everything that happens in the higher and lower worlds is as a result of man's actions. It is mankind who affects the activity in worlds beyond.

We are obligated to recognize our great potential, not for the sake of arrogance, but rather to serve Hashem to our fullest ability and to save ourselves from sin. For when a person recognizes that, *"Bishvili nivra ha'olam* – the whole world was created for me (*Sanhedrin* 37a),"*, inasmuch as through one's spiritual growth and his ability of *yichud haleiv*, he can transcend nature and affect higher spheres, he will never want to sin. Rather, he will feel exalted and inspired to run to serve Hashem in truth. May we be privileged to experience the fulfillment of our prayer, *"Veyacheid Levaveinu* - And You (G-d) should unify our hearts to love and fear you...until eternity."

Not So Fast

The Drill Sergeant was dismissing his men when he casually mentioned to Goldberg, "By the way, Goldberg, your best friend just got killed in action."

The Lieutenant, having observed the Sergeant's insensitivity, called him to task and blasted him for his callousness.

The next day, the Sergeant received word that Goldberg's grandmother had passed away. Before he dismissed his men, he yelled out, "Hey, Goldberg, your grandma kicked the bucket this morning!"

Again, the Sergeant was sharply rebuked by his commanding officer for his insensitivity.

A week later, the Sergeant was about to dismiss his men when he was handed a telegram in regard to the sudden passing of Goldberg's father. Not wishing to be reprimanded by the Lieutenant again, he blurted out, "Men! Now listen here! All those who have both parents living, take one step forward! Not so fast, Goldberg!"

Avraham Avinu somehow had the ability to withstand the difficult test of the *akeidah* and actually proceed on that mission, anxious as he was to fulfill the word of Hashem. In contrast, Sarah Imeinu, who had a greater level of prophecy than her husband, nevertheless could not bear the news that her son had been placed on the altar, a heartbeat away from death. This discrepancy can be explained by virtue of the way they were made aware of the *akeidah*. Avraham was instructed: *"Take now your son, your only one, whom you love, Yitzchak."* (Bereishis 22:2) Rashi explains the subtleties of this *passuk*: "Your son" – He [Avraham] said to Him, "I have two sons." "Your only son" – He said to Him, "Each one is singular to his mother." "The one whom you love" – He said to Him, "I love them both." [Then He said,] "Yitzchak is the one I mean." Rashi continues: And why didn't Hashem just tell him this from the beginning? Hashem wanted to avoid giving a sudden command, lest Avraham be accused of complying in a state of confusion and disorientation.

A simpler explanation might be that Hashem allowed Avraham the few moments in between each expression to enable him to adjust to the precarious situation at hand. By the time he understood that he was to sacrifice Yitzchak, he had been partially prepared for the task. Sarah, on the other hand, who was informed of the *akeidah* by the Satan in a sudden and abrupt manner, was unprepared for the shock that her beloved son was about to be slaughtered, and her soul left her.

With the passage of each moment, man has the uncanny ability to acclimate himself to the most dire of situations. People who survived various disasters and upheavals will tell you that their survival rested on their ability to adapt. Those who survived the horrors of the Nazi concentration camps certainly invoked this *middah* as a key to their forbearance and ultimate survival. Without the ability to adapt, we would find it impossible to endure our ever-changing lives.

The Gemara teaches that one should not be the bearer of bad news. With the various examples that the Gemara then brings, it is clear that *Chazal* are not only stressing the importance of sensitivity regarding such delicate matters, but are also giving advice on how to convey such news, so that its recipient can absorb it and adapt to it in a gradual fashion. By being somewhat indirect and vague, the news is absorbed in increments, which allows for the necessary adjustment of the person. Such is the nature of man.

However, this very character trait, which allows for man's survival, is at times his biggest undoing. Precious moments of inspiration are lost, indelible impressions fade away, because man adapts so well – too well! And although that too is human nature, man must work steadfastly to ensure that he remains an inspired individual and not succumb to the malaise of "old hat" and complacency.

The prophet Yechezkel instructed Klal Yisrael that they never exit the Beis Hamikdash the same way they entered. The Yaavatz explains that the purpose of this instruction was to ensure that a person never become as familiar with the Beis Hamikdash as he was with the walls of his home. Familiarity breeds comfort, which in turn suffocates any spark of inspiration. How, then, does one remain inspired, when routine wears away at those sparks that have been stirred, rendering them unremarkable and typical?

There was a Jew by the name of Palti ben Layish who merited special Heavenly intervention that allowed him to escape a dreadful sin. The daughter of King Shaul was betrothed to Dovid through a *kiddushin* that Shaul held to be invalid. Deeming her to be unmarried, Shaul proceeded to marry her off to Palti, who understood that his new "wife" was quite possibly an *eishis ish* (married woman). This was indeed the position of Dovid, who held that his *kiddushin* was halachically valid. Palti made a decision then and there that he would not touch this woman (his new "wife"). In order to concretize his commitment, he thrust a sword between the two of them and asserted, "Whoever (referring to himself) involves himself with this woman, shall be pierced by this sword." It was due to this noble act that he merited tremendous *siyata d'Shmaya* and was able to escape a grave transgression.

What exactly was so great about Palti thrusting a sword into the bed between them? Was that really going to prevent him from becoming intimate with this woman in the almost inevitable eventuality of his *yetzer* overwhelming him, during the many years they were together? All he'd need to do would be to remove the sword, go around the sword, or just simply ignore it. What practical purpose did it serve, and why did this act warrant such *siyata d'Shmaya*?

Harav Chaim Shmulevitz *zt"l* explains that herein lies a fundamental concept that is worthy of internalization. Palti knew that his momentary determination and steadfast commitment would not last forever. He knew that many a weak moment would befall him on the road ahead. He needed to do something to physically express his sincere conviction at that moment, to act as a perpetual reminder that there was a time when he had felt so strongly about this matter and had possessed the strength to overcome all obstacles. In the spirit of the *passuk*, "Im ta'iru v'im t'orraru es ha'ahavah ad she'techpatz – If you awaken or arouse the love while it is desirous," (*Shir Hashirim* 3:5) which alludes to the fact that one needs to take inspiration and immediately transpose it into a physical object (*"techpatz"* being of the same root as the word *"cheifetz* – object"), Palti thrust all of his determination into that *cheifetz* – the sword – and declared: If I should ever dare to touch my new wife, I shall be worthy of death. And at moments of weakness, I will look at that sword, the symbol of my strength, and be able to revert back to that auspicious moment of lucidity and spiritedness. I will be reminded of the strength that I once possessed, and will become reinvigorated to withstand the temptation. And in doing so, I will have defeated the malady of adaptation, my flame reignited, my confidence restored.

Palti's genius was the revelation that we don't have to succumb to the malady of familiarity and routine; that those priceless moments of inspiration need not be lost. We can re-connect to them and regain that spiritual energy. When those treasured moments come our way, we pray that they not dissipate, but instead linger. Let them jar our memory, to be recalled and reignited, and to leave us indelibly inspired as before. Inspiration might be fleeting and dissolve all too fast, but its spirit remains, never too late to retrieve.

To Tell the Truth

The two elderly gentlemen, Harry and Isaac, were sitting in their doctor's waiting room, sharing information about their aches and pains, when they realized that each one had the exact same symptoms in his foot. When Harry was called in, Isaac, remaining in the waiting room, listened intently, anxious to hear his friend's fate. Blood-curdling screams were heard coming from the examining room, making Isaac even more anxious. Finally, Harry came out, and Isaac was called in. Harry, curious to see if Isaac's treatment would cause as much excruciating pain as his did, decided to wait for his friend so that they could share notes. Two minutes later, Isaac was back in the waiting room, smiling from ear to ear.

"I don't get it!" said Harry. "We seem to be suffering from the same ailment, yet my treatment was so painful and yours was a breeze!"

"Harry," whispered Isaac, "do you think for a moment, that after listening to you scream in there for half an hour, I showed the doctor the right foot?"

It's not easy to admit the truth. We're not particularly good at it, for many reasons. We are surrounded by, and submerged in, a world of falsehood that inevitably takes its toll on even the most well-meaning amongst us. From the political spectacle of unkept promises and sensational hype, to the lack of commitment and fidelity of our most sacred relationships, man has time and again shown himself to be nothing more than a self-serving fraud. How distant we are from the great *talmidei chachamim* and *tzaddikim* of the past, whose steadfast and unrelenting commitment to *emes* – truth was inextricably linked to their close attachment to the *Ribono Shel Olam*, the Source of all that is true. In striving to emulate Hashem, whose very signet and crowning symbol is truth, they pursued *emes* with alacrity and fled from anything that threatened their integrity.

The Gemara says that *tzaddikim* cherish their money even more than their physical existence, the reason being not their enchantment with money, but rather their love of honesty and integrity and their pursuit of truth that went into its acquisition.

How far we are from the Chiddushei Harim *zt"l*, who once told two *misnagidishe gedolim*, (The *geonei hador* R' Akiva Eiger and R' Yaakov M'lisa), who were visiting the Chemdas Shlomo and who wanted to honor him with a piece of cake late one morning before he had *davened* Shacharis, "*Ich ess nisht kein lekach* - I don't eat cake." (Since he hadn't *davened* yet, he couldn't eat the cake.) His intent was to avoid mentioning the practice of Gerrer chassidim at that time, which was to *daven* later in the morning. He thought that it might not be understood, and thereby would be an affront to the honor of the *roshei yeshivah*. Nonetheless, rest assured that since those words came out of his mouth, he was absolutely committed to uphold them, and not eat cake for the rest of his life.

How removed we are from Rav Yaakov Kaminetsky *zt"l*, who did not eat *gebrokts* for the remainder of his life after telling the family where he was assigned to eat one Pesach, that he was stringent in *gebrokts*, simply in order to avoid a dubious kashrus situation.

How remote from us is the story of the great *gaon* Harav Aharon Kotler *zt"l*, who would not permit the yeshivah to use stationery with a logo of the planned building construction, because of extraneous bushes drawn into the design by the architect in order to enhance the picture.

These were natural responses for Jews of this caliber, so closely attached to the Source of all truth. We, however, find ourselves entrenched in a society where the rule of thumb, at times, is to "out-lie" the other guy. Too often, it's the one who manipulates and maneuvers the best who wins. How difficult it is, then, to admit to the truth, when we are so seasoned in denial.

I'm reminded of the story of a woman who hears a radio report warning drivers and pedestrians about a mentally-unbalanced man who is driving down the boulevard the wrong way. Concerned for her husband, who often takes that route, she immediately calls him on his cell phone.

"Hi! Listen, I just heard on the radio that there's a crazy guy driving down the boulevard the wrong way! Please be careful!"

"What do you mean, a crazy guy?" the husband responds. "Why, there are hundreds of them!"

I used to think this was a humorous story until I once mistakenly made a left turn into the wrong lane of traffic and suddenly found dozens of cars coming at me at fifty miles an hour. It was quite frightening! I just pressed on the horn and hoped for the best. But what I found even more disconcerting was that my initial reaction was to wonder why all those cars were going the wrong way, until it hit me that it was I who was on the wrong side of the road.

My ninth-grade English teacher gave off an aura of confidence and assuredness mixed with a little pomposity and arrogance. He would boast: "I was wrong only one time in my life. I once thought I was wrong, when I really was right!"

We have a hard time being wrong in a world that preaches state-of-the-art perfection and that it's not important whether you win or lose, as long as you win! Who could admit to the truth when admitting one's mistakes is associated with failure and imperfection? And when you add to the equation a global malaise caused by low self-esteem, admitting our indiscretions becomes emotionally unbearable.

In addition, our general approach to things that are broken is to throw them out rather than fix them. So why even begin the process of "fixing" by admitting our mistakes, when it is an effort in futility? It's been said humorously that there was a man from Los Angeles who had a watch that was always three hours fast. Rather than fix it, he moved to New York.

Unfortunately, we've become a throw-away society, where appliances are made to break, and leftovers are deemed inedible simply because they've spent the night in the refrigerator. Much to our chagrin, however, we cannot simply throw out our old selves and buy new ones. We need to begin the process of being intellectually honest and introspective, with the greatest of integrity. If we don't, we will never grow, we will never change, and most certainly, we will never do *teshuvah*.

The question is asked why the sin of the Golden Calf was forgiven, while the sin of the spies was not. To this very day, we suffer from the effects of the sin of the spies, as the ninth of Av, the day of the spies' slanderous report, became a day of potential calamity for all future generations. The Baal Shem Tov explained that the difference between the two sins lies in the aspect of being *modeh al ha'emes* – admitting to the truth. When Moshe Rabbeinu pleaded with Hashem to forgive Klal Yisrael for the sin of the Golden Calf, his plea was replete with their admission that they had sinned, as it says, *"And Moshe returned to Hashem and he said, 'Indeed this nation has sinned a great sin.'"* (*Shemos* 32:31) In contrast, the spies were not so forthcoming about their error. They said: *"Behold we went up to the place (Eretz Yisrael) about which Hashem has said we have sinned."* (*Bamidbar* 14:40) They never could admit their sin. The best they could do was to acquiesce that the *Ribono Shel Olam* considered their report a grave error. And because they could not admit their guilt, they could not be forgiven.

It is told that in a certain town where the Jews were victimized by various anti-Semitic decrees, the community accepted upon itself, not a fast day, nor a day of prayer, but thirty days of accepting reproach without uttering a word of defense or response. For thirty days, everyone was to be *modeh al ha'emes*, to admit and to absorb, and to allow constructive criticism to penetrate their hearts. What greater show of willingness to change could there be than to begin the process by connecting to the truth. The stage is then set for sincere reform, and earnest and solemn repentance.

Shalom Bayis - The Home

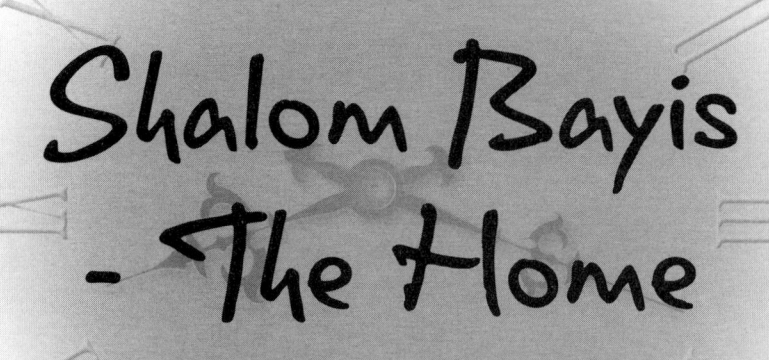

Home Sweet Home

"**D**on't forget we are moving today. If you come home to this house this afternoon, it will be empty!" Professor Jones's wife said to her absent-minded husband.

Predictably, the professor forgot all about it, and returned to the vacated house that afternoon, without any recollection whatsoever as to where it was that his family had moved. He went outside to the front of the house, where he found a little girl playing.

"Excuse me! Did you happen to see a moving van parked in front of this house today?" he asked.

"Yes," she replied.

"Do you remember what time it was here?" he asked.

"I think it was around three this afternoon." she replied.

"Would you happen to know which way it went?" he asked.

Looking up at him, she answered, "Yes, Daddy, I'll show you exactly where it went!"

People who are on their best behavior in the company of others, at a workplace, school or supermarket, will let down all barriers in the comfort of their homes. This idea that someone with a sterling reputation in the eyes of others could act and speak coarsely to his own wife and children is an anomaly that requires explanation. Does he not remember that these are his precious loved ones who are his best friends and most devoted advocates? Does he suddenly draw a blank on all the devotion, dedication and *nachas* they have brought him? What prompts him to speak and act so gently and properly outside of his home, while at home, he sometimes resembles a raving madman? The same person who puts in an effort to strike the proper balance in his interpersonal conduct, can be totally off-balance, as he lets his hair down in, of all places, his home. Even those who have the sensitivity to turn their homes into a sanctuary, and preserve its dignity by restricting its content to things that are *kadosh* – holy – can somehow forget to include proper *middos* and *derech eretz* in speech and deed, to that endeavor. The self-control and discipline that sustains the person who is outwardly a *mentsch* can get lost in the clutter of the homestead. How can this happen?

"It's human nature," we can say. "Everyone's like that!" We concern ourselves with the impression we make on others and how we will appear in their eyes, when in truth, our conduct will have its deepest effect on those closest to us. One way or another, that behavior pattern will come back to haunt us. Children learn through osmosis. Our outbursts could one day become theirs. Our choice of words might very well become part of their vernacular. It is frightening to see our children repeat our mistakes, especially when we were their inspiration. In the heat of an argument we might speak to our spouses in tones that would be unthinkable if it were a disagreement with others. In the end, we hurt those who are closest to us in a pervading and penetrating way. It may be human nature, but it is unacceptable for a Torah Jew.

When Rav Yochanan Ben Zakkai was on his deathbed, his *talmidim* came to visit him. (*Brachos* 28b) They asked him for a *brachah*. He complied and said: "*Yehi ratzon shetehei mora Shamayim aleichem k'mora basar v'dam* – May it be Hashem's will that the fear of Heaven should be upon you like the fear of mankind." The *talmidim* then asked, "*Ad kan* – That's all, and no more?" meaning to ask, shouldn't the fear of Heaven be greater? Rav Yochanan responded; "*U'levai!* – If it were only so!" meaning that while the importance of fearing G-d may be greater, in actuality it would be a step up if it were even equal. R' Yochanan brought a proof to his point since when a person commits a transgression in private, he says "I pray that no one will see me." How foolish we are to fear mankind more than the All-seeing, the All-knowing omnipresent G-d.

This distortion of reality carries over to our social behavior in the privacy of our homes. In that setting, safe from outside observers, we feel unfettered of the fear of others. We can be ourselves! If only we would act at home the way we act in front of others. *U'levai,* that our interaction with our family members would be treated with the same scrutiny and sensitivity as with friends and associates. Surely, we know that there is no privacy that excludes the *Ribono Shel Olam*, no domain free of His presence. And if there is one place in particular that we welcome Him, it is into our homes that we attempt to transform into a comfortable abode for the *Shechinah*. There is no excuse for absent-mindedness, rather we must know and appreciate where we live, with whom we live, and make that abode the model for all that is good.

Sailing the Seven C's of Chinuch

The Hebrew school teacher was projecting her own heretical views, when she asked her class if they really believed that Jonah was swallowed by a whale and survived. Little Sarah, unabashed, was brave enough to respond:

"Yes! I believe every word of it!"

"Well, how will you prove that it is true?" the dissident teacher asked.

Sarah, not hesitating for a moment, answered, "When I get to Heaven, I'm going to ask Jonah myself!"

"But how do you know that Jonah is in Heaven?" asked the teacher. "Maybe he's in the other place."

Sarah didn't flinch. "Then you ask him!"

Children are bright, resourceful, and quite perceptive, very often putting us adults to shame. One thing is for sure: Any parent or teacher who thinks for a moment that he is "merely dealing with a child" underestimates and misunderstands the "absorbent sponge" and pure-minded phenomenon that stands before him. Everything we do and say will be soaked up by this precious child, either through his unusual sharp senses, or through the process of osmosis. We adults must always be on our best behavior, lest our children's lasting impressions of us come back to haunt us one day!

1) **CONDUCT:** Ours! The way we act and conduct our lives will reflect immeasurably on our children and students. A father who sets aside time to learn Torah regularly, who makes sure to be *ma'avir sedra*, who makes his Shabbos table a memorable occasion, replete with words of Torah, *hartzig zemiros*, and, perhaps most important, warm and *geshmak* conversation with his children, will reap the rewards of his efforts. A mother who talks softly, even when things are tense, who is careful about her mode of dress and modesty, who opens her home to guests and involves herself in community needs, who showers her family with motherly tenderness, will find that her mark has been made on her children in the most unobtrusive and natural way. A couple who speaks respectfully to one another even when in disagreement, whose shared love and devotion is apparent in word and in deed, whose relationship is built upon mutual respect,

openhandedness, selflessness, and self-sacrifice, will merit to see children who build homes founded on *shalom* and tranquility. Children who are privileged to grow up in a home where *shalosh seudos* and *melaveh malkah* are not mere extras, where *lashon hara* is never an option, where a disparaging word about the Rabbi's speech or the neighbor's lawn is nonexistent, where the talk in the home is positive and upbeat, filled with praise and encouragement, where there is an outpouring of love and affection among family members, will soak up that atmosphere and have it infused into their blood forever.

Imagine the impression it makes upon children who see their parents *bentch* from a *bentcher* and answer their phone calls instead of instructing the one who picks up the phone to "tell them I'm not home;" their father running out late at night to catch a midnight *minyan* for Maariv; their a mother trying to *daven* Shacharis and Minchah. How fortunate is the child who grows up in an environment of great enthusiasm for *mitzvos*, where *tzedakah* is given with joy and generosity, where the glory of the *Ribono Shel Olam* and the magnificent world He created is spoken about without inhibition, where the flaunting of an ostentatious and pretentious lifestyle is abhorred, no matter what one's fiscal status. When our conduct will be on par, we will merit to see the diffusion of all that we hold dear, in our greatest treasure – our precious children.

2) **COGNIZANCE:** An awareness of the greatness of the gift of children is essential in the *chinuch* process. In

a world that has decided that children are a hassle and interfere with its chosen self-serving or career-consuming lifestyle, we must be unequivocal about the priority we place on our progeny and their development. We are here to toil and to build our own small world, and our children and grandchildren are the pillar and backbone of that edifice. Every ounce of energy and resources that we invest into our children will enhance that structure and enable us to build that world. *Chazal* compare one who is not blessed with children *r"l* to a dead person, for one's children are his life, his future, and the object of his purpose on this earth. Children allow us to fulfill our innate and natural inclination and yearning to give, as we give to that which we helped create, having been granted the privilege of collaborating with the Creator of all that exists, in a partnership for posterity. Children allow us the opportunity to imitate and emulate the *Ribono Shel Olam*, albeit in a miniscule way, in the manner in which He continuously sustains life. And it goes without saying that they are the source of our greatest *nachas* and joy, which fills our hearts with even more love for them. Each child is a precious gift from Hashem, for which we are eternally grateful.

3) **CUDDLING:** We must display our love for our children by showering them with tenderness. Our warm embrace, our demonstrative show of affection, encourages and secures a bond that is not easily broken. There is no limit to the amount of love and encouragement we can give our children. This should be our general demeanor, notwithstanding the importance of discipline, which is

also a show of love. Compliments and the accentuation of the positive should be the creed of our interaction with our children. Criticism should be carefully lined in silk, and given only at the appropriate moment. We should remember that our children are always our "babies" who need the cuddling and the comfort contact of those who have nurtured their growth. As I think back to my own parents *z"l*, I realize that even as a fully grown middle-aged man, I so miss their warm hugs and kisses, the strength they constantly infused in me.

Our children must be told how much we love and cherish them, how each one is special and unique. Never should they doubt our belief in them, for they look to us for strength. We dare not disappoint them.

4) **"CAVOD" (KAVOD)** – honor: You may be thinking: Give honor to your kids? You must be kidding! Not in the least! Harav Avraham Pam *zt"l*, who was exemplary in the *middah* of giving honor to others, writes in his *sefer*, *Atarah L'melech*: "To embarrass a Jewish person is a violation of a Torah precept. This includes minors as well." Although there surely are occasions that warrant discipline, for the sake of the *chinuch* of the child, one must be aware of the repercussions of his actions. Unfortunately, it is all too common for the damage caused by inappropriate disciplinary methods to exceed the benefits. "One could achieve much more by following the path of showing honor and gentleness."

A child is a real person with real feelings that should be handled with utmost sensitivity. Although he more readily accepts his fate as a member of the "small" community, the build-up of incessantly being squashed and disrespected can take its toll. The teenager whose opinion is just pushed under the rug or written off as some uncontrollable hormonal whim, without discussion or explanation, will likely be heard saying, "My parents hate me." This may very well mean, "My parents don't respect me."

There is no question that discipline and direction are crucial to every child's development, but there is a major difference between imposed despotism that dehumanizes, and mutually respectful instruction that builds a person's character. When dealing with students who are lax about their class attendance, I first tell them how much I missed them in their absence. Then I ask them to explain their non-attendance. The message is clear: "I'm concerned about your lapses, but I haven't lost my love and respect for you." Children must feel our respect for them, and this itself will teach them a tremendous lesson in *kibbud av v'eim*.

5) **CONSOLATION:** Our children need to know that they can turn to us for everything. We need to engage them in conversation and spend time *shmoozing* with them, in order to establish a rapport and create an open line of communication. The developing of trust between parent and child is essential to the level of impact a parent's words might have upon his children. The Gemara encourages marrying off one's children at a young age when they will still entertain their parents' suggestions.

As with any relationship, the degree to which a child will seek his parents' council is directly linked to their level of mutual trust and respect. Although our children are not our peers, they should be made to feel the bond of our unlimited friendship and our listening ear. Children should find in their parents the comfort they seek to allay their fears and the solace needed to ease their tension. In the healthiest of parent-child relationships, the parent never ceases to be a parent, and remains that special source of consolation and strength to his children of any age.

6) **CRISIS MANAGEMENT:** At times we need to ride the storm and do our best at maintaining stability and equilibrium. No matter how many books one reads on *chinuch*, nobody is the perfect parent, and mistakes are inevitable. Certainly, the teenage years present the greatest challenge, with damage control often becoming the focus, more so than instruction and direction. At times of crisis, it is crucial that we keep the lines of communication open, and display our genuine love and concern overtly. We need to come to terms with the wisdom of losing the battle to win the war. Our objectives remain the same. Sometimes, though, it takes a little longer to get there.

7) **"C"(S)IYATA D'SHMAYA:** We must *daven*. I will never forget the tears and heartfelt cries of my dear mother *z"l* as she *bentched licht*. We must *daven* that Hashem grant us the wisdom to say the right thing at the right time, and more importantly, not to say the wrong thing

at the wrong time; that we control our anger; that we not allow our personal frustrations and moods to interfere with the commonsensical approach so crucial in *chinuch habanim*; that an atmosphere of *shalom* and *simchah* pervades our homes, providing the security and warmth to nurture our children's optimal growth; that their hearts should be open to *yiras Shamayim* and love of Hashem; and that Hashem bestow upon our children all of His blessings.

The Bar Mitzvah – The Bar Chiyuvah

The Reform rabbi and the priest were comparing notes about a mutual problem shared by both of their congregations. Both of their places of worship had been overrun with rodents. The priest was at his wits' end, having tried every exterminator in town, with no success. The rabbi, on the other hand, had easily licked the problem.

"How did you do it, Rabbi?" asked the priest. "Why, I've used every exterminator in the book, with no luck at all!"

"I use a different method," answered the rabbi. "I gather all those critters together in the main sanctuary, take out the Torah scroll, and give them

a bar mitzvah. You can bet your bottom dollar that it will be the last time I'll see those fellas in Temple!"

How sad it is when the beginning of becoming a *bar chiyuva* (man of responsibility), instead, turns into the beginning of the end. Fortunately, among *ehrliche Yidden*, the bar mitzvah marks the humble beginnings of what promises to be an illustrious career for one who joins ranks with those privileged to serve their Creator and do His bidding. How gratifying it is to observe the novice *bar chiyuva* as he takes on his new obligations with zest and enthusiasm, and with a degree of maturity beyond his years. All the while, his parents and siblings are wondering, "Who is this young adult with the hat on his head, doing all these adult things like *leining*, *davening* for the *amud*, and saying his *p'shetl* as if he was a *rosh yeshivah* giving the *shiur klalli* to the entire *beis medrash*?!" What happened to that little kid with the squeaky voice? It's almost as if he entered a new world!

In fact, he did! This bar mitzvah boy became a new entity. He's now called a *bar chiyuva* and is obligated in all 613 commandments.

The very source for a *seudas* bar mitzvah (celebrating the bar mitzvah with a festive meal), is a statement said by Rav Yosef, who was blind, that were he to be convinced that the halachah concurred with the opinion that a blind person is obligated in *mitzvos*, he would make a feast for the rabbis. This celebration would be built upon the understanding that, "*Gadol hametzuveh v'oseh mi'mi she'eino metzuveh v'oseh* – Greater is the one who is commanded to do something and does it, than the one who does it voluntarily." Contrary to a more popular notion that one who performs voluntarily is even more worthy of reward, *Chazal* teach us that the *metzuveh v'oseh* – the one who is commanded to do something and does it, the *bar chiyuva*, is greater. One of the many explanations for this teaching is that the *metzuveh v'oseh* is in sync with the preferred manner of performing all *mitzvos* – as a servant fulfilling the king's command. The person's action is not motivated by his emotions or by something that appeals to his intellect; it is not because his compassion is stirred, nor is it done simply to satisfy some personal whim to feel spiritually fulfilled. His action is much more pure and pristine. It is for the sole reason that the King of all kings, *Hakadosh Baruch Hu*, has so decreed.

This idea is illuminated in a Rashi in *Brachos* (33). The *mishnah* castigates one who lavishes praise upon Hashem for the compassion shown to the mother bird in the mitzvah of *shiluach hakein*. The mishnah says: If one proclaims, "How merciful You are, Hashem, in that Your compassion even extends to the bird's nest," we silence him! We tell him, in no uncertain terms, that such statements reflect a distortion of what *mitzvos* are all about.

In the words of one Amora's explanation of the mishnah, the person is intimating in his prayer that Hashem's *mitzvos* serve the purpose of showing His great sensitivity for His creations, when in fact their purpose is to make it known that we are His servants and the devoted keepers of His decrees.

Rashi's words are unequivocal: "The purpose of *mitzvos* is not to proclaim Hashem's great compassion, but rather to place upon Klal Yisrael the laws of His decrees, to make it known that they are His servants who guard His *mitzvos*, His decrees, and His laws, even with regard to matters that the Satan or the nations of the world might decry as unnecessary and meaningless." All *mitzvos*, whether they appeal to our senses or not, should be observed because the King of all kings has commanded us to do them, and we humble ourselves to His will because they are the *gezeiros hamelech*.

In this lies the greatness of the *metzuveh v'oseh*, and the advantage thereof. The bar mitzvah, the fresh *bar chiyuva*, is now privileged to fulfill *mitzvos* in the most ideal sense: as a servant of Hashem fulfilling his Master's decree. No longer are *mitzvos* a matter of rational choice or voluntary selection, but rather they are elevated to the realm of a person humbling himself before his Creator.

The bar mitzvah festivities celebrate the sublime joy one experiences when the *Ribono Shel Olam's* will and his own are one and the same. It is indeed worthy of a "feast for the rabbis," for it is the *talmidei chachamim* who personify this creed, and therefore nothing could be a more fitting celebration than a *seudah* with their participation.

I'll never forget my son, Chaim's, bar mitzvah in the fall of 2001. My father, Rav Yaakov Kurland *zt"l*, who was very weak and ill, a victim of a horrific car accident three years before, somehow was able to attend the *simchah*. It was just a week or two after the monumental calamity of 9/11. The world was still in a state of shock, their security jolted. My father, frail and fragile from his own personal upheaval, spoke a few simple but penetrating words from the wheelchair to which he was confined. He said:

"Tonight, not only has the bar mitzvah *bachur* become a *bar chiyuva*, but the whole world has become a *bar chiyuva!*"

We attend many a bar mitzvah celebration, to the point where it can become humdrum and monotonous. What inspiration should we draw from these occasions? We should become reinvigorated in our *avodas* Hashem, with the zest and vitality of the young and fresh bar mitzvah *bachur*, privileged to join the rank and file of humble servants of Hashem, and ennobled with the distinction of being a *metzuveh v'oseh* and a *bar chiyuva*.

Tefillah

Keep on Shuckeling

Bugzie Goldberg, a notorious crook, was incarcerated at a maximum security facility for fifty years to life. His crimes included grand larceny, auto theft, kidnapping, breaking and entering, attempted murder, and murder in the first degree. One day, he received a letter from his aging father, filled with expressions of his unconditional love for his son, as well as his overwhelming loneliness:

"Dear Son,

I miss you so terribly! I remember so fondly how you and I would go outside this time of year, to prepare the vegetable garden for planting. We'd plow up the ground, and sow the seeds, and sit back and watch them grow. Oh, how I long for those days. Now I'm left to do it all on my own.

All My Love, Dad."

A few days later, Mr. Goldberg received a letter from his son Bugzie in prison:

"*Dear Dad,*

Whatever you do, don't dig up the garden! That's where I buried all the bodies."

The very next day, two vans pulled up at the old man's home, and ten FBI agents exited with shovels in their hands. For the next few hours, they proceeded to dig up every inch of that garden, but found absolutely nothing but dirt.

Two days later, the old man received another letter from his son in jail:

"*Dear Dad,*

By now the garden should be all dug up and ready for planting. It was the best I could do under the circumstances.

All My Love, Bugzie."

One of the many gifts we Jews have been privileged to receive as part of our heritage is the concept of never giving up. No matter the circumstances, we are steadfast in our belief that, "Even if a sharp sword is pointed at one's neck (and seemingly the end is near), he should not give up hope but should continue to implore Hashem's mercy." (Brachos 10)

Yitzchak Avinu established the prayer of Minchah. This is based on the *passuk*: "*Vayeitzei Yitzchak lasuach basadeh* – Yitzchak went out to pray in the field." (*Bereishis* 24:63) The numerical value of the word "*siach* – prayer" is 318, which is one more than the word "*yiush* – to relinquish hope," which is 317. As long as a Jew can pray, he never gives up hope. Instead, he picks up his head and prays again, as the *passuk* instructs, "*Kavei el Hashem, chazak v'ameitz libecha v'kavei el Hashem* – Hope to Hashem, be strong and He will give you courage; and hope to Hashem."

A person once complained to the Ponevezher Rav that he was *davening* and *davening* for a particular matter, but he felt that Hashem was not listening. The Rav told him, "Hashem is definitely listening, but for the time being, the answer is 'no.'" Often the answer is "not yet," but we must never become discouraged.

We must continue to *daven* with the conviction that *tefillos* are never wasted. One *tefillah* pulls in another. At the appropriate moment, they will find their mark; they will make their impression, and the *Ribono Shel Olam* will respond. So keep *davening*! Don't stop! And in the process of doing so, one will find himself developing an ongoing, intimate relationship with his Creator.

It is a grave error to think that one's prayers don't help or aren't accepted because of his sins. It isn't uncommon for one to believe that Hashem despises him, but this is nothing more than a tactic of the *yetzer hara*, who would like us to believe that we are unworthy. The very nature of *tefillah* is such, that if uttered with sincerity, it will ultimately penetrate all barriers (at times with the help of other *tefillos*), and it will be effective in bringing the desired results. For some, it may take one *tefillah*; for others, many more. Moshe Rabbeinu *davened* 515 *tefillos* – the numerical value of the word "*Va'eschanan* – and I prayed" – to be allowed entry into Eretz Yisrael. But then he had to be told to stop, for otherwise his *tefillos* would have succeeded, and Hashem would have been "forced," as it were, to grant Moshe his wish. Obviously, the *Ribono Shel Olam* had a different calculation, but as far as Moshe's *tefillos* were concerned, his persistence had paid off; his *tefillos* finally had achieved their goal.

Imagine the despair that could have been felt by Chizkiyahu Hamelech, who, upon his deathbed, was visited by Yeshayahu Hanavi and told, "You will die in this world, and you won't live in the World to Come [either], because you never married." Chizkiyahu certainly believed Yeshayahu to be a *navi emes*, a true emissary of Hashem, whose words were prophetic and spoken with absolute *ruach hakodesh*. Nonetheless, Chizkiyahu commanded, "End your prophecy and leave! For I have a tradition from my father's house (Dovid Hamelech), that even a sword threatening one's life, or even the words of a true prophet, should not deter a person from praying to Hashem." Immediately, Chizkiyahu turned to the wall and *davened* for his life that hung in the balance, and he was rewarded with fifteen more years.

We make the mistake of thinking that the *Ribono Shel Olam* conducts His world with two distinct *hanhagos* (methods): one in the realm of *teva* (nature), and the other in the realm of *nissim* (the miraculous). This is merely our distorted perception, aided by the facade of a well-disguised, seemingly nature-run world. However, nothing could be further from the truth. To the *Ribono Shel Olam*, there is absolutely no difference between the two *hanahgos*. *Everything* in existence is wondrous and miraculous! Hashem is "*mechadeish b'chol yom tamid ma'aseh Bereishis* – He renews and recreates, every day, always, the act of Creation." He breathes life into our every breath – miracle of miracles!

The numerical value of Hashem's Name *"Elokim"* is 86, which is equal to *"hateva* – the nature," for the world of Heaven and the world of earth is one marvelous, Providential domain, where anything is possible, if willed by Hashem. Therefore, we never relinquish hope, and we never give up, because we believe with complete faith the words of the *passuk*, *"Hayi'palei me'Hashem davar*– Is there anything too wondrous for Hashem?" Certainly not! So I will never stop *davening*. I will keep on *"shuckeling,"* and in doing so, I will be an impressive display of *"Kol atzmosai tomarnah, Hashem mi kamocha* – All my limbs will say, Hashem, who is like You?" (*Tehillim* 35:10)

Tefillah: It's Not Just Three Times A Day

Barry, a secular Jew, was running late for his job interview in Manhattan. Nervously, he circled the streets looking for parking, berating himself for not leaving home earlier. He couldn't afford to lose this opportunity. As the 9:00 a.m. interview approached, in desperation, with only a few minutes to spare, he offered a prayer to Heaven:

"G-d, if You help me find a parking place, I promise I'll go to synagogue every Saturday!"

Suddenly, a car pulls out of its slot right in front of the office building he needs to enter. Barry swiftly pulls in and says, "Forget about it, G-d! I found a spot myself!"

Prayer, as understood in the secular world, is reserved for emergency situations, when one's options have run out, and there is nowhere else to turn. Even authentic Jews, at times, view *tefillah* as a three-time-a-day obligation, to be completed within a specific time framework. And although that is true, we would be terribly remiss if we were to stop there without uncovering its genuine meaning and purpose and unparalleled worthiness.

The Gemara in *Shabbos* (10a) refers to *tefillah* as "*chayei sha'ah* – living for the moment," in comparison to Torah which is "*chayei olam* – living for eternity." In contradistinction to Torah, which is our link to eternity, *tefillah* deals with the basics of this world: food, health, peace, etc. Perhaps we can suggest a deeper explanation for why *tefillah* is referred to as "*chayei sha'ah*."

The Gemara in *Brachos* (6a) describes *tefillah* as something that stands "*berumo shel olam* – in the highest places of the universe," and yet people are "*mezalzelin bahem* – they denigrate its true value." Through *tefillah*, one can reach a level of *hispashtus hagashmius*, the shedding of all earthliness, that allows one's intellect to soar to heights close to prophecy. (*Shulchan Aruch Orach Chaim* 98:1) Clearly, *tefillah* is not simply about asking for one's physical needs. It is about the creating of an intimate bond with one's Creator.

This relationship ideally develops into an ongoing conversation with the *Ribono Shel Olam,* a give and take, a debate, a discussion, a negotiation of sorts, a dialogue between a Jew and his Father in Heaven. In the *passuk* (*Yeshayahu* 1:18) "*Lechu na v'nivachecha yomar Hashem,*" Yeshayahu Hanavi calls it a "*vikuach* – deliberation" that is in progress twenty-four hours a day, in no way restricted to Shacharis, Minchah, and Maariv.

"*Vayeitzei Yitzchak lasuach basadeh* – And Yitzchak went out to meditate in the field (*Bereishis* 24:63)." The Gemara in *Brachos* (26b) points out that the word "*lasuach*" could be interpreted as "to *daven*," for its root word, *siach* (lit. conversing), is an expression of *tefillah*. Indeed, conversing is the very nucleus of *tefillah*. A continuum of numerous, nonexclusive communications and conversations between man and his Creator, lies at the very core of this unique medium of *avodas* Hashem.

How clearly do the words of my wife's Bubby Rissel *zt"l*, a uniquely pure *tzadekes*, ring in my ears! "Hashem is my friend. I speak to Him." Her *tefillah* relationship was without interruption, part of her uniform routine. It most certainly was not confined to time periods alone, but rather, it was an ever-present reality that she lived with every day. Like Dovid Hamelech, who described himself as one perpetual prayer, we need to tune in to Hashem's accessibility every moment of the day.

The numerical value of the word "*siach*," which is 318, is one more than "*yiush* – despair," which is 317. This reiterates the idea that Hashem is accessible 24/7, no appointments necessary, no waiting, all insurances accepted. There is no place for hopelessness; absolutely no room for despair.

The *Mesillas Yesharim* (ch. 19), in describing the magnificent opportunity of *tefillah*, writes so poignantly: "However, an intelligent person with a little contemplation and focus, can establish the truth of this matter in his heart, how he actually comes and converses with Hashem may He be blessed, and actually offers his supplication before Him, and personally beseeches Him. And that Hashem, may His name be blessed, listens and pays close attention to his words, just as a man speaks to his friend and his friend gives him his undivided attention."

In the same vein we understand the Gemara's statement (*Brachos* 28b), "If one makes *davening* a ritual of rote performance and commonplace routine, his prayer has no appeal." It has no attractiveness or charm. It has no *chein* (favor), because it was a prayer of obligation only, and not of intimacy. It was a prayer of duty, and not one of closeness and affinity.

The *vikuach* of *tefillah* helps the one who is praying clarify his priorities. Through the give and take of his multiple conversations with his Confidant, as it were, the *Ribono Shel Olam*, he is able to remove the inessential and focus on his primary needs. It is like one who confides in his best friend, revealing his heart and exposing his worries and concerns, uncertain of what exactly it is that is really disconcerting, only to find clarity from his loving friend's insightfulness, or simply by having had the opportunity to talk it out to a caring, listening ear. Similarly, through his dialogue with Hashem, the person is able to make an honest appraisal of his requests, having sifted through his thoughts in the course of conversation with the Source of all that is true, *Hakadosh Baruch Hu*.

Perhaps, *tefillah* is referred to as "*chayei sha'ah*" to make this very point. We live and breathe *tefillah* every hour, every minute. At every moment of need for expression, it is available. The *Ribono Shel Olam* is there for us with no time constraints. He is my Friend; He is my Beloved; He always cares; He's always listening. I'm never disturbing Him; He always has time for me. He is my Father; He is my Mother. We have an intimate relationship twenty-four hours a day, seven days a week, nonstop. He will never forsake me! Now that's praying!

The World We Live In

Deadheads

Steve got off the train at the wrong stop, on a dark, dreary fall afternoon, the first day after the clock was pushed back. The early arrival of nightfall, coupled with the dangerous neighborhood, made him quite anxious, to say the least. He decided to get back to familiar ground as soon as possible by taking a shortcut through a cemetery.

Needless to say, the eeriness of the graveyard made him even more uneasy. He was therefore thrilled to see an old man walking ahead. Quickening his pace, he soon caught up with the old fellow. He anxiously related how relieved he was to have company to walk with because, "Quite frankly, I'm scared out of my wits."

The old man slowly turned to him and said, "Son, I understand completely. Why, if I was alive, I'd be plenty scared myself!"

A well-known musical group, *The Grateful Dead*, had fans so devoted that these fans would travel around the country to attend every concert. Neither distance nor expense would deter them. These fanatical followers earned the title of "Deadheads." Unfortunately, we live in a society replete with deadheads, many of whom have no musical appreciation whatsoever. They are the *living* dead of the Gemara (*Brachos* 18) that says, "The wicked are called dead, even while they are alive."

Not only is the living dead a real concept, it is unfortunately a very prevalent one. Consider how society at large is preoccupied with living for the moment. This promotes a self-serving existence that renders one incapable of focusing on others, an existence that is devoid of G-d or any thought of eternity. It becomes clear why we are surrounded by the living dead.

On the other hand, the same Gemara contrasts the wicked, who are considered dead, with the righteous: "The righteous, even after their deaths, are called (as) alive." How much more alive is a *tzaddik* while he still breathes! The life of the aspiring *tzaddik* is alive and vibrant. Every second is precious; every moment is an opportunity; every challenge is a potential victory; every action is a link to eternity.

The *passuk says*: "*V'Avraham zakein ba bayamim* – And Avraham was old; he had come along in years. " (*Bereishis* 24:1) Rashi interprets the redundancy of "*ba bayamim* – he had come along in years" to mean: "All of his years came with him."

A similar thought is expressed in regard to Sarah Imeinu. The *passuk* says, "And the life of Sarah was one hundred years, and twenty years, and seven years; the years of the life of Sarah." (*Bereishis* 23:1) In explanation of the unusual breakdown of the years of Sarah's life, and the repetition of the word "years," Rashi comments: "All of [the years] were equal in their goodness."

Harav Chaim Shmulevitz *zt"l* elucidates the implication of Rashi's words. Avraham and Sarah shared the outlook on life that every moment was a potential brick; a brick upon which they could place another brick, in an effort to construct an edifice, an *olam hakatan* – a miniature world, to be eternalized forever. All of Avraham's years came with him, because each day was built upon the day before it. All of Sarah's years were equal in their goodness, because all her years were equally essential to help amass her version of a grand world of accomplishment that she could call her own.

Eisav, the quintessential *rasha's* name, is an expression of *asui* – already done. His name implies that he was a finished product even before he started. Edom, another name by which Eisav was known, connotes *demamah* – silence, intimating the lifeless nature of this *rasha*. He was born physically matured, (*Bereishis* 25: 25) equating the concept of the *rasha* with the stagnation of growth and development. He is described as "*ish sadeh* – a man of the field," which *Targum Onkelos* translates (elaborated by *Tosfos* in *Bava Kama* 92b) as "still and wasted" – null and void, empty and bankrupt, limp and lifeless – a deadhead at his best.

In sharp contrast, Yaakov Avinu's title, which is parallel to Eisav's, is "*yosheiv ohalim*," (*Bereishis* 25:27) translated by *Targum Yonasan Ben Uziel* as "one who pursues greatness." One who is full of vitality, vision, and purpose strives for completeness in this world and the next. Yaakov's entire *raison d'etre* was to live eternally, to the point where the Torah's report of his demise is introduced with the words, "*Vayechi Yaakov* – And Yaakov lived." (*Bereishis* 47:28)

Chazal emphatically state (*Taanis* 5b): "*Yaakov Avinu lo meis* – Yaakov our father never died," and nor does any Jew who lives the ideal of his lineage. We stand proud and privileged to be part of such a legacy; to be among the living, attached to the Source of all life.

Life Insurance

An eighty-year-old man enters an insurance agency in Tel Aviv and tells the clerk he wishes to purchase life insurance. The clerk, trying to hold back his laughter, tells the old man, "You're too old; we don't sell life insurance to a person your age."

Unflinching, the old man says, "Well, two weeks ago you sold life insurance to my father."

"Your father! You must be kidding! How old is your father?"

"He's 108, *biz a hundred und tzvanzig yohr* (until 120 years), may he live and be well," replies the elder statesman.

"If you insist, I'll look it up, but I highly doubt it ... One minute, you're right! I guess it's only fair that we sell you a policy as well. Can you come in next Tuesday for a physical?"

"Next Tuesday? No, I'm afraid I can't. You see, my grandfather is getting married next Tuesday!"

"Let me get this straight," says the incredulous clerk. "Your grandfather is getting married next Tuesday. My gosh, how old is your grandfather?"

"My grandfather is 132 (*biz a hundred und tzvanzig yohr*)."

"Your grandfather is 132 years old, and he's getting married next Tuesday? Can I ask you one more question? Why in the world did he wait so long?"

"Ah...! His parents are giving him a hard time!"

From time memorial, man has yearned to uncover the secret to longevity. Advances are made every day in medicine and technology that are increasing life expectancy. Emphasis on fitness, exercising, body-building, and dieting has become the routine for many, in their ongoing effort to maintain their youthful appearance and physical health. We have become a society who will undergo whatever ordeal necessary in order to shorten our nose, brighten our smile, remove our need for unflattering eyeglasses, and the like. Cosmetic surgery helps contribute to the myth that we can defy mortality and live forever.

But deep down, we all know the truth. The end is inevitable, and, unfortunately, by then, the person who has chased after youth all his life will have wasted the precious years of his life, dreaming the impossible dream.

Not so for the *Yid* who views the world from spectacles of eternity. He knows that life does go on forever. He understands that man is a composite of a body and a soul, and he strives to earn his eternity, not in some abstract, fictitious, and frivolous manner, but in a structured, deliberate, and concrete program of Torah and *mitzvos*, *chessed* and *tzedakah*, and *middos tovos* and character refinement, that will accrue merits for him, allowing him to truly live forever.

We say in the blessings of Shema in Maariv: "*Ki heim chayeinu v'orech yameinu* – [Torah] is our life and the length of our days." It is through Torah and *mitzvos* that we are capable of living everlastingly. Hashem placed the fountain of youth and the secret of life in our very laps. The rest is up to us and no one is giving us a hard time.

Torah

Never the Same

It was quite intriguing that the name of the Chinese proprietor of the local dry cleaners was Abe Schwartz. When someone finally worked up the courage to ask him about the origin of his name, Mr. Schwartz explained:

"When I came over to this country, the man who stood in front of me in line at Immigration was a Jewish man named Abe Schwartz. When my turn came and they asked my name, I told them the name my parents had given me – Sem Ting."

It is well-known that of all of the *mitzvos*, the study of Torah reigns supreme. Our learning is something we hold on to for dear life, for it is our life. Yet, if our learning is of the "it goes in one ear and then out the other" variety, it loses its vitality both from the perspective of its effect and of its reward. We desperately need to learn the importance of *chazarah* (review) as the mainstay of the fulfillment of learning Torah. This is where we often encounter the "Same Thing Syndrome."

The "Same Thing Syndrome" is an ailment that affects many who, to their credit, may study Torah regularly, but suffer from the attitude of, "I've learned that before; I can't learn it again. I must learn something new, something I've never learned before. There's so much to learn, I don't have time to review."

Chazal tell us that just the opposite is true. They explain, regarding what appears to be a redundancy in the *passuk* of "*Im shamo'a tishma* – If you will surely listen (*Devarim* 11:13)," that if you learn the old information well (through constant review), then the new information will be understood that much more easily. The acquisition of the old studies, through the toil of constant *chazarah*, will not only facilitate the acquisition of the new studies with greater ease, but will bring a surge of *siyata d'Shmaya* that will make the unfathomable his, and the unreachable within his grasp.

The importance of review underscores the ultimate goal of Torah study, which is *kinyan haTorah* – the acquisition of Torah. Our task is not merely to study Torah, but to acquire it, to make it ours. In discussing the issue of whether a *talmid chacham* has the right to be *mochel* on his *kavod* (relinquish the honor he is due), the Gemara (*Kiddushin* 32) attempts to bring a proof for such a right from the *Ribono Shel Olam* Himself, Who so humbly acted as a personal guide for Bnei Yisrael in the desert. The Gemara immediately objects that we can't learn from Hashem's willingness to yield His honor, because the world is His and the Torah is His, and therefore its honor is within His jurisdiction to concede, as opposed to the *talmid chacham* who has no such dominion. Rava responds that indeed the honor of the Torah *is* the *talmid chacham's* to renounce, for the Torah is his once he learns it repeatedly and has acquired it. At first, it is the Torah of Hashem, but after a concerted effort on the part of the Torah scholar to acquire his learning, it becomes his. The true *talmid chacham* takes his Torah with him wherever he goes, for it is his, embedded in his mind and implanted in his heart.

Chazal teach us in *Brachos* (6:) "*Igra dipirka rihata* - The primary reward for the studying of Torah at the *shiur*, is for the energy expended in running to the *shiur*." The question is conspicuous: Shouldn't the primary reward for the study of Torah be for the study of Torah itself? Rashi Hakadosh once again comes to the rescue. He explains why the primary reward is the reward for running to the *drasha* and not the *s'char limud*. The reason is "S*heharei ruban einam meivinim* - that most of the people attending the *shiur* do not understand the *drasha* well enough to remember its text; so as to repeat it properly in the name of their *rebbi* at a later date, for which they would have received the more cherished reward for the learning of Torah." Rashi's words are monumental yet frightening. To think that the most coveted reward we seek is so easily lost without proper retention! This places a great responsibility upon us to acquire our learning so that it is inscribed in our memory bank, secured for eternity.

The Gemara in *Brachos* (32) discusses the *chassidim harishonim* – early righteous ones, who would spend nine hours a day involved in prayer. The Gemara questions the limits that this practice would place on their time to learn Torah. But the Gemara never asks the more obvious question, when did they have time to learn? Rather it asks: "*Torasan heich mishtameres* – How did they retain their Torah?" How was their Torah guarded in their memories, when they had so little time to review what they had learned? (*Maharsha ibid*.) The *gemara's* focus is on their *kinyan haTorah*, for that is primary.

Purim and Chanukah are the exclusive *yamim tovim D'rabanan*, rabbinically instituted holidays, which help pave the way for our survival in *galus*, bridging the gap until the coming of Mashiach. Each of these *yamim tovim* in its own way, focuses on Torah. The amazing revelation on Purim brought about an accepting of the Torah out of Klal Yisrael's love for Hashem and His miracles, an acceptance that that surpassed the one at Har Sinai (*Chazal* say that the Jews, *hadar kibluhah* - *voluntarily* re-accepted the Torah after the story of *Megillas Esther*). Through the events of Chanukah; the *Torah shebaal peh*, the oral law, became ever more prominent as the panacea to protect against the forgetting of Torah until this very day.

The unusual ecumenical acceptance of the *mehadrin min hamehadrin* – the most glorified manner of performing the *mitzvah* of lighting Chanukah candles, may very well be linked to the idea that Klal Yisrael didn't *really* require a miracle when they wanted to re-inaugurate the Menorah. After all, the law is *tumah hutrah b'tzibur* – if the majority of the people are contaminated, the laws of spiritual impurity are relaxed. In addition, there is no absolute requirement for the thickness of the wicks. The victorious Jews could have used the impure oil, or have made the wicks 7/8 thinner so as to burn less oil, until new oil could be procured. The one reason that they did not, was that to use such oil would have detracted from the beauty of the *mitzvah*. Because the entire miracle of Chanukah came about because of their insistence to be *mehader b'mitzvos*, to beautify the *mitzvah*, there evolved the universal commitment to perform this mitzvah like the *mehadrin min hamehadrin*, in the most preferred and enhanced fashion.

If Chanukah marks the beginning of the power of the light of the *Torah shebaal peh* to illuminate the darkness of the impending *galus* through the *pilpulah shel* Torah, as well as a time when the enhancement of a *mitzvah* played a pivotal role in the events of the day, then it is a time when we must focus on how to be *mehader* – enhance our study of Torah. What greater *hiddur* could there be in the learning of Torah, than the constant review of Torah? Indeed in Aramaic the word *mehader* means to return, to review.

Perhaps this too is the meaning of the *Chazal* regarding Klal Yisrael's re-acceptance of the Torah after the story of Purim. *Hadar Kibluhah* - The *Kabbalas Hatorah* of Purim was one of *hadar*, meaning review. The clarity they enjoyed and their love for Hashem and His Torah that ensued from the miracle of Purim, inspired them to accept upon themselves to learn Torah with an absolute commitment to make it theirs forever.

Through the *kinyan haTorah* – the acquisition of what we learn, we can take the Torah we've learned into the darkness of *galus* with a renewed confidence that it will protect us in this world, and be our delight in the World to Come.

The "Chein" of the Plain and the Humble

Harvey finally had settled into the hot bath that his aching back so sorely needed, when the doorbell rang. At last, he had a bit of a respite in that steamy, soothing tub, and he was in no mood to be disturbed. Grumpily, he got out of the bath, put on his robe and slippers, and went downstairs to answer the door. "I'm coming, I'm coming!" he yelled out in an exasperated tone, as he made his way to the door. To his annoyance, it was some rabbi from Israel at the door, asking for a donation for a yeshivah that Harvey had never heard of. Harvey fished out a dollar to rid himself of the nuisance, and ran upstairs as fast as he could, anxious to get back into that relaxing tub.

Seconds later, the doorbell rang again. Annoyed again, Harvey climbed out of the tub, put on his robe and slippers, and started for the door, irate at this second disturbance. A salesman wanted to know if he needed any brushes. Harvey, having lost his patience, slammed the door in the man's face, and returned to the bath.

In a matter of seconds, the doorbell rang again. Harvey, beside himself, angrily climbed out of the tub, but this time he slipped on the wet floor, flipped into the air, and landed squarely on his back, against the hard porcelain bathtub. Cursing under his breath and wincing in pain, he scrambled to his feet, threw on some clothes, and racked by riveting spasms, drove himself to the doctor.

After examining him, the doctor said, "You're very lucky. Nothing seems to be broken. Not even a hairline fracture. But you seem very tense. You need to relax! Why don't you go home and take a long hot bath?"

The great Hillel Hazakein was faced with a similar dilemma, but his response was so refined and aristocratic. The Gemara in *Meseches Shabbos* (31a) describes in great detail a wager made between two men, one insisting that he could incite the anger of the patient and humble Hillel.

It was Erev Shabbos in the afternoon, and Hillel was bathing in preparation for Shabbos. His peace was disturbed by a boisterous voice, irreverently screaming out without a hint of respect for the *nasi*: "Is Hillel here? Is Hillel here?" Hillel quickly dressed and descended; then patiently attended to his visitor.

"How can I help you, my son?" Hillel asked warmly, without any trace of annoyance.

"I must ask you this question," his visitor responded.

With great forbearance, Hillel said, "Ask my son, [please] ask."

"Why are the heads of the Babylonians elongated?" the man asked. Not exactly an earth-shattering question in halachah.

"You have asked a very important question," Hillel said encouragingly. "It is because their midwives are not adept in the birthing process."

Hillel returned to the bath, but the same series of events repeated themselves. Each time, Hillel dressed and descended, unperturbed by this nuisance, and patiently addressed the trivial questions posed. "Why do the Tarmudaim people have rounded eyes? Why do the Africans have such wide feet?" the questioner asked, forcing the sage to leave the comfort of his Shabbos preparations a second and third time.

"The Tarmudaim people's eyes protect them from the frequent sandstorms that plague their deserts, and the Africans' wide feet prevent them from sinking into the swamplands that typify that country's topography," Hillel answered wisely. Needless to say, the questioner lost the bet, because the great Hillel would not be provoked in any way.

One could well imagine how bothered we might be by such unnecessary infractions on our privacy. What was Hillel's secret? The Gemara's introductory statement to the above story is: "A person should strive to have the patience of Hillel." The choice of adjective used is "*anvesan* – patience," easily associated with "*anivus* – humility." That is the underlying secret. The true *anav* (humble person) can tolerate all situations that come his way, because intolerance is inextricably linked to a big ego, and the *anav*'s ego is low-spirited and humbled. Hillel's patience was a natural outgrowth of his unpretentious nature that maximized the *chashivus* of others.

It would be hard to imagine a *gaon* greater than Rav Akiva Eiger *zt"l*, and yet his brilliance in learning was matched by his brilliance in humility. In the introduction to his *Teshuvos* – Responsa – he apologizes if he referred to his students as *talmidim*, reasoning that he had learned more from them than they had from him. Is there anything more beautiful than the combination of absolute mastery in Torah together with inviolable humility? How fortunate were we, of this generation, to have seen the aggregated erudition of a *gaon* like Harav Moshe Feinstein *zt"l*, and at the same time to have witnessed the genius of his *pashtus,* simplicity! The same R' Moshe who completed the study of *Shas* and *Shulchan Aruch* hundreds of times, devoted time on a regular basis to help a woman who lived in his building translate the letters that she received from her relatives in Russia. Such a combination is a marvel to behold. It is a symphonic display of greatness and simplicity that is distinctively characteristic of *gedolei Yisrael*.

There is a gift from Heaven that attaches itself to the humble. There is a charm and a charisma that characterizes the modest, and makes them attractive and alluring. It is a "strand of c*hessed*" that descends upon them from above. It is what made a Hillel Hazakein the beloved leader of Klal Yisrael whom all revered. It is what made R' Akiva Eiger the *rosh yeshivah* of all *roshei yeshivah*, and Rav Moshe Feinstein the *sar haTorah* – officer of Torah of our generation. It is the gift of *chein* (favor).

Shlomo Hamelech taught us that there are two types of people who are granted this gift. One group is the humble.

"*U'l'anavim yitein chein* – To the humble will be given the gift of *chein*." (*Mishlei* 3:44) The other group is people who study Torah, the *talmidei chachamim*, as it says, "*[Torah and mussar, absorbed into one's spiritual bloodstream,] are adornments and ornaments of chein.*" (*Mishlei* 1:9) It is a gift that speaks volumes about the *nachas* and appreciation that the *Ribono Shel Olam* receives from the *anav*, humble person, and the *talmid chacham*, Torah scholar, respectively, let alone the glorious symphony of the two together. It is because of the fusion of simplicity and greatness that they merit this special gift of favor from the One above, which in turn endears them to the masses of Klal Yisrael. May we be privileged to be "*mis'abek b'afar ragleihem* – revel in the dust of their (the scholars') feet," for even the dust of their feet is holy.

Turn A Shiur Into a Prayer

It was the High Holiday season, and Seymour had never gotten around to purchasing a seat in the shul. He didn't have that much interest in attending anyway. On the first day of Rosh Hashanah, he needed to get an urgent message to his father, who was a steady shul-attendee. Seymour ran to the entrance of the shul, only to be stopped at the door by the *gabbai*.

"Where do you think you're going?" scolded the *gabbai*. "You can't enter the Sanctuary unless you've purchased a seat and have a ticket!"

"I didn't buy a seat this year," answered Seymour, "but I only want to go in for a minute to give an urgent message to my father."

"Okay," said the *gabbai* reluctantly. "I'll let you in just for a minute. But I better not catch you *davening*!"

Davening is not the only way to communicate with our Creator. Learning Torah, besides its obvious cerebral qualities, is also a medium of communication with the *Ribono Shel Olam*, which calls out and beckons and breeds a bond of intimacy with the Giver of the Torah. In the process of studying Hashem's Torah, one becomes familiar with the very vernacular of the Creator of the universe Himself, and this forms a unique resonance and rapport between man and G-d, unlike any other. As the person articulates the symphony of a *"shakla v'tarya"* (Talmudic give and take), he sings the *shira* - song that is replete with praises and thanks to the *Ribono Shel Olam* for sharing with him His holy Torah. As one fine-tunes his understanding of the intricacies of the *sugya* and its halachic ramifications, he offers a silent prayer to the *Ribono Shel Olam* to grant him the *yiras Shamayim* to adhere to His laws in every detail. As a child or a novice plows through his first *blatt* of Gemara, making note of every word and nuance, a prayer is expressed for *siyata d'Shmaya* and continued strength to rise to the challenges that learning in a foreign language and skill-building can bring. At the same time, the learner implores *Shamayim* for more inspiration, so that he, too, can join the rank and file of *talmidei chachamim* and *yirei* Hashem.

Rav Tzadok Hakohen from Lublin points out that the very source for reciting the *birchos haTorah* before learning Torah, is a *passuk* that defines the study of Torah as an act of calling out to Hashem. The *passuk* says: "When I will call out the Name of Hashem (when I will study Torah, which is a conglomerate of many combinations of the Names of Hashem [– Maharsha]), I will [first] speak of our G-d's greatness [by making a blessing]." Clearly, learning Torah is referred to as "calling out to Hashem."

Continuing on this theme, Rav Tzadok quotes the Gemara (*Brachos* 3) that attempts to reconcile an apparent contradiction in two *pesukim* of *Tehillim*. One *passuk* says, "At midnight I (Dovid Hamelech) arise to thank You for Your judgments that are righteous." (*Tehillim* 119:62) A second *passuk* says, "I arose at twilight, vashavaya - and I cried out to You." (ibid. 119:147) When did Dovid Hamelech rise? Was it at midnight, or was it at twilight? One answer the Gemara suggests is that he got up at twilight and learned Torah until midnight. Then he sang songs of praise to Hashem until dawn. This means that the *passuk* of "*I arose at twilight and I cried out to You,*" is referring to the study of Torah. "*Shav'ah* – crying out," one of the classic expressions for a heartfelt prayer that emanates from the very recesses of one's soul, is used to represent the Torah learning of Dovid Hamelech. Is there any doubt that through the study of Torah, one engages, as well, in effective prayer, enhancing his close connection to Hashem?

Another possible proof for Torah study being a way to connect to Hashem, and thus a form of prayer, is the *passuk:* "*Toras Hashem temimah mishivas nafesh* – The Torah of Hashem is perfect, restoring the soul." (ibid. 19:8) The word "*nafesh* – soul" can also be understood as an expression of prayer, as used by none other than Chana, the mother of Shmuel Hanavi, from whom many *halachos* of *tefillah* are learned. She said, "*V'eshpoch es nafshi lifnei Hashem* – And I poured out my soul before Hashem," (*Shmuel I* 1:15) in her explanation to Eli Hakohen for the unusual anguish in her heartbreaking plea for a child. Using this definition of the word *"nafesh,"* as a term for prayer, we can understand the above *passuk* from *Tehillim* to be describing Torah as something that is so perfect and all-encompassing, to the point that it even incorporates *tefillah* – prayer into its essence. *"Mishivas* – restoring" can be understood as an expression of response or communication. So Torah study is *"mishivas nafesh"* – a communication of prayer, which indeed restores the soul.

From the day that the Beis Hamikdash was destroyed, all that remains of significance to *Hakadosh Baruch Hu* are the *"daled amos shel halachah bilvad* – four cubits of halachah alone." Sadly, we presently do not enjoy the privilege of a Beis Hamikdash in our midst and the tremendous benefits thereof. We don't have the advantage of fully-accessible, open gates of prayer, like we used to have. But we still have the *"daled amos shel halachah."* We still have the Torah that has the quality of containing everything within it, as it says, *"Hafoch bah, hafoch bah* - Deliberate over it again and again, for everything is contained within it." (*Avos* 5:22) And part of that which is within Torah is the powerful tool to implore Hashem that He rebuild the Beis Hamikdash speedily in our days, amen.

Sources and Outlines

Introduction: A Time to Laugh, a Time to Listen

Communication comes in different forms, and is not restricted to verbal articulation.

Story - Rav Aharon Kotler, Rav Avraham Kalmanowitz and Rabbi Shlomo Shapiro. Vaad Hatzolah - Rav Aharon's Yiddish was well understood simply by virtue of the passion in his voice.

True communication doesn't involve words as much as the opening of the heart.

The universal language of humor, a medium of expression that breaks down barriers.

Shabbos 30 - (*milsah d'bidichusah*) - it systematically removes all the *mechitzos* that can otherwise immobilize the lines of communication.

Koheles 8:15 - "ושבחתי אני את השמחה"-the joy of performing a mitzvah like *hachnasas kallah*.

Shabbos 30 - וכן לדבר הלכה

Rashi ibid. - צריך לפתוח במילתא דבדיחותא ברישא

Shabbos ibid. - כי הא דרבה מקמי דפתח להו לרבנן אמר מילתא דבדיחותא ובדחי רבנן

Rashi ibid. - נפתח לבם מחמת השמחה

Shabbos ibid. - לסוף יתיב באימתא ופתח בשמעתא

The relationship between שמחה and צמיחה (מפי מו"ר הרב שלמה פריפלד)

Melachim II 3:15 - "ועתה קח לי מנגן" (Elisha and Yehoshafat) for the Divine Spirit to rest upon him, Elisha Hanavi first needed to expand, to accommodate it.

Avos 5:7 - "עומדים צפופים ומשתחוים רווחים" - stretching and expanding - the essence of the Bais Hamikdash, to transcend earthly limitations.

Making oneself into a miniature Bais Hamikdash to house the *Shechinah*, the *Shechinah* can only rest where there is *simchah*.

Eiruvin 3 - אלא הללו שוחקות והללו עצבות (טפח שוחק-טפח עצב), the "happy" *tefach* is a wider measure.

Expanding to become the most absorbent receptacle possible through *simchah*.

Between Man and G-D

Fear of Heaven: It's Yours for the Asking - *Yearning for yiras Shamayim*

Bernie in Heaven, for just the two of us it doesn't pay to cook.

The difficulty of becoming a *yirei Shamayim* in a world that champions the free spirit.

Devarim 10:12 - "ועתה ישראל מה ה' אלקיך שואל מעמך כי אם ליראה את ה' אלקיך" וכו'

Brochos 33 - וכי יראת שמים מילתא זוטרתא היא / אין לגבי משה מילתא זוטרתא היא?

Did Moshe Rabbeinu not understand the pulse of the people and their difficulty with *yiras Shamayim* thereof?

Indeed, *yiras Shamayim* is a *milsah zutrasah* - for everyone to attain.

Brachos 33 - הכל בידי שמים חוץ מיראת שמים

Amud Ha'emes (Kotzker) p 137 - it refers to the realm of *tefillah*.

Rosh Chodesh *bentching*- "ויראת חטא" בהם יראת שמים ויראת חטא" - *yiras ha'onesh v'yiras haromimus*

Heard in the name of Rav Leib Gurwitz, Rosh Hayeshiva of Gateshead- *Chaim sheyesh bahem ahavas Torah v'(ahavas)yiras Shamayim*, a yearning for *yiras Shamayim*.

Our problem is that we don't really crave it.

"*Shoel mei-imach*"-"*ki im l'yirah*"-for *yiras Shamayim* to be in the realm of "*ki im* ("simply") it requires ("*shoel mei-imach*") sincere prayer from within.

• • •

Has Anyone Seen My Father? - The legacy of Yaakov Avinu as the quintessential *mevakeish Hashem*

Circus job, head in lion's mouth, looking for my father.

Taanis 5 - *Yaakov Avinu lo meis*, coming in contact with our congenital capacity.

Bereishis 25:27 - "איש תם"-the essence of Yaakov Avinu was that he was a *mevakeish Hashem*.

Targum Yonosan Ben Uziel 25:27 - "תבע אולפין"

Shemos 33:7 - "כל מבקש ה'"

Targum Unkelos ibid. - תבע אולפין.

Story - *Gvir* and *rosh yeshiva* with a *shidduch* proposal (please don't go until you tell us the answer).

Story - Rav Chaim Shmuelevitz, Rav Avraham Yoffin, the Steipler Gaon - the *mevakeish*, the best *bachur* in the yeshivah.

Bumper stickers of yesteryear - "I ain't even looking for it."

Divrei Hayomim I 16:9 - "ישמח לב מבקשי ה'"

• • •

I Don't Even Know You - "והבוטח בה' חסד יסובבנו"

Mugger, a check? I don't even know you.

The global meltdown and resulting worldwide lack of trust, the crash of 2008-2009 has weakened man's resolve to work harmoniously with mutual confidence.

Bava kama 8 - זה נהנה וזה לא חסר

Tehillim 146:3 - "אל תבטחו בנדיבים"

Tehillim 146:5 - "אשרי שקל יעקב בעזרו"

Parnassah b'gematria neshamah.

Tehillim 145:16 - "פותח את ידיך ומשביע לכל חי רצון"

Tehillim 32:10 - "והבוטח בה' חסד יסובבנו"

Devarim 8:17 - "כחי ועוצם ידי עשה לי את החיל הזה"

Beitzah 16 - כל מזונותיו של אדם קצובים לו מראש השנה ועד יום הכיפורים וכו'

Taanis 8 - כמה גדולים בעלי אמנה

The story of the weasel and the pit - *bitachon* empowers.

Taanis 8 - אין הגשמים יורדים אלא בשביל בעלי אמנה

Tehillim 68:35 – "תנו עוז לאלקים"

Kli Yakar Vayikra 25:36 - The severity of the *issur* of *ribbis* is that it encroaches on one's *bitachon*.

The "get rich quick" philosophy.

Kesubos 33 - הכל בידי שמים חוץ מיראת שמים

Brachos 30 - הכל בידי שמים חוץ מצנים ופחים

Yeshayah 1:3 - "ידע שור קוניהו חמור אבוס בעליו ישראל לא ידע"

• • •

It Ain't Just Luck - Accruing *zechuyos*

Steve's lucky day - she came in seventh.

The zodiac mindset.

Shabbos 156 - אין מזל לישראל, our privileged relationship with Hashem extends beyond the world of *mazel*.

עכו"ם-עובדי כוכבים ומזלות

Sanhedrin 3:3 - משחק בקוביא פסול לעדות - he is preoccupied with the foolishness of chance when his investments should be in futures.

Shabbos 32 - Rav Yannai - protecting one's *zechuyos* - לעולם אל יעמד אדם במקום סכנה לומר שעושין לו נס שמא אין עושין לו נס, אם עושין לו נס מנכין לו מזכויותיו

Bereishis 32:1 "קטנתי מכל החסדים" - the creed of *tzaddikim*.

E-ZPass philosophy of life, taking chances just for the thrill of it.

Haggadah - echad mi yodeia - Kotzker - who knows the reason for the creation of the number one?

Zohar Hakadosh Terumah 161- איסתכל באורייתא וברא עלמא קודשא בריך הוא - the Torah as the blueprint for creation.

• • •

Sing His Praises O' You Nations - The hidden salvation

Two elderly women, Sadie and Mildred, on a Sunday drive.

Living in oblivion, unaware of our protection.

Tehillim 118:10-11 - "כל גוים סבבוני בשם ה' כי אמילם. סבוני גם סבבוני בשם ה' כי אמילם"

Our preoccupation with the need for the *yeshuah*, causes us to be unmindful of the many on-going *yeshuos*.

Tehillim 117:1-2 - "הללו את ה' כל גוים שבחוהו כל האומים כי גבר עלינו חסדו ואמת ה' לעולם הללוקה"

Why should (would) the goyim praise Hashem for his kindness to Klal Yisrael?

Tehillim 2:1-4 - "למה רגשו גוים ולאומים יהגו ריק יתיצבו מלכי ארץ ורוזנים נוסדו יחד על ה' ועל משיחו. ננתקה את מוסרותימו ונשליכה ממנו עבותימו. יושב בשמים ישחק ה' ילעג למו"

We may be ignorant of all of their plots and the ensuing salvation, but they, surely are not, and ironically are forced to praise Hashem.

Between Man and Himself

Oblivious - אין אדם רואה נגעי עצמו

Marty and Sadie - fishing trip, note, it's 5:00 a.m.

Negaim 2:5 - אין אדם רואה נגעי עצמו – subjectivity.

Negius - loshon negah - like a plague.

Michtav M'Eliyahu Vol. 2 p 202-203 Parshas Chayei Sarah.

Bereishis 24:5 - "אולי לא תאבה האשה ללכת אחרי... ההשב אשיב את בנך וכו'"

Bereishis 24:39 - "ויאמר אל אדני אֻלַי לא תלך האשה אחרי" - *ulai*-spelled *chaser* can be read אֵלַי-to me, implying subjectivity.

Wouldn't Eliezer be more likely to have *negius* in the initial conversation before seeing Divine *simanim* that Yitzchak's *bashert* was indeed Rivka? Why is the word written *chaser* (אלי) in the second conversation?

Negius is so overwhelming, it precludes the possibility of any awareness or cognizance of its presence. Eliezer's oblivion was a product of the power of *negius*.

"כי השוחד יעור עיני חכמים ויסלף דברי צדיקים" - *Devarim* 16:19

• • •

Priorities - Relinquishing one's heart

Superbowl, empty seat, they all went to the funeral.

The many loves of life.

Sanhedrin 74 - *sugya* of "*yehareig v'al ya'avor*"

Brachos 54 - "בכל נפשך"- אפילו נוטל את נפשך

Devarim 6:5 - "ואהבת את ה' אלקיך בכל לבבך ובכל נפשך ובכל מאדך"

Chidushei Harim Al HaTorah Parshas Va'eschanan - אפילו - "בכל לבבך" נוטל את לבבך - giving up one's heart.

The *mesiras nefesh* of our *dor* might be *mesiras halev*.

Tehillim 119:92 - "לולי תורתך" - without establishing the priority of Torah - "אז אבדתי בעניי" - in the pain of not knowing what to emphasize.

• • •

What's in a Name? - Finding one's *shoresh neshamah*

Presidential candidate visiting nursing home, old lady, do you know my name, ask at the front desk.

Yoma 83 - ר׳ מאיר מדייק בשמה

Bris liturgy - כשם שנכנס לברית, the *ruach hakodesh* in naming a child.

Makkos 4 - שלא השם המביא לידי מכות מביא לידי תשלומין,- the name meaning the *shoresh*, the source

שם בגימטריא׳ מקר-340

Assimilation in name and loss of perspective of one's personal mandate from Hashem.

Neos Hadeshe Vol. 1 *daf* 197 - no שומע כעונה by *sefiras haomer* - each individual must count on his own.

The individual *chelek* in Torah of each member of Klal Yisrael.

Midrash Shir Hashirim - ישראל an acronym for יש ששים רבוא אותיות לתורה

Bereishis Rabbah 2:5 - "כתבו לכם על קרן השור שאין לכם חלק באלוקי ישראל"

Koheles 7:1 - "טוב שם משמן טוב"

Avos 4:17 - "וכתר שם טוב עולה על גביהן"

Mishlei 6:23 - "כי נר מצוה ותורה אור"

Mishlei 20:27 - "נר ה׳ נשמת אדם"

Mishlei 4:2 - "כי לקח טוב נתתי לכם תורת אל תעזובו"-Torah is called "טוב"

Koheles 7:1 - "טוב שם משמן טוב" - one comes into contact with his name, his true essence through the Torah.

Between Man and His Fellowman

Everybody Counts - I Don't Get No Respect - Looking at the potential

Ice-skating on the frozen pond, wait till the weather warms up, no respect.

Everyone needs respect.

Bamidbar 1:1- Rashi ibid. - The counting of *Klal Yisroel* מתוך חבתן מנאן

Beitzah 3 - *Davar sheb'minyan lo botil*, Hashem counted us to give us distinction.

Bava Metziah 85 - Rebbi gave *semichah* to the son of R' Elazar ben R' Shimon who had strayed from the path (כל זונה שנשכרת בשתים שוכרתו בשמונה) he restored his *chashivus*.

Story - Rabbi Aryeh Levin, Rabbi Shmuel Aharon Yudelevich, spoke to him in the third person from bar mitzvah age.

Avos 2:10, 2:13 - 5 *talmidim* of Rabi Yochanan Ben Zakkai and their unique attributes.

רואה את הנולד seems out of place.

It is the foundation of the other *middos* - by seeing the potential greatness of others, he achieves the other four *middos*.

Story - Rabbi Shlomo Heiman, the *shiur* for future generations

• • •

Giving, Never Taking - אַ גוט מארגען אַ גוט יאר

Bank loan, car as collateral, back in a week, $25 interest, where can you get parking in Manhattan for $25.

A "what's in it for me society".

Brachos 10 - Shmuel Hanavi wouldn't be *neheneh* from others.

Chulin 7 - R' Pinchus ben Yair and Rebbi, "גבה טורא ביניייהו" - *Shamayim* interceded to allow him to maintain his *hanhagah* of not benefiting from others-מימיו לא בצע על פרוסה שאינו שלו ומיום שעמד על דעתו לא נהנה מסעודת אביו

Elisha, Isha Hashunamis - he accepted her hospitality.

Mieri in *Brachos* 10 - his intention was to repay her for her graciousness.

Two reasons for their *hanhagah*: 1. Not to become subservient to anyone but Hashem. 2. Not to become a taker.

The "*tzu kumt mir*" attitude that prevails today.

Rabbi Shlomo Freifeld- "*ah gut morgen a gut yahr*"-people always gave back more.

Eiruvin 54 - Story of Rav Preidah and the *talmid* he taught 400 times - an incredible demonstration of giving - הב דעתך ואתני לך / הדר אתני ליה ד' מאה זימני

Chasam Sofer - *hakdamah* to *Teshuvos* - learning with others, *siyata d'Shmaya*.

Megila 6 - לאוקמי גירסא סייעתא מן שמיא היא

Avraham would not take from the king of Sedom.

Story – Kelm, the Alter bought the right to bring the water, young boy, R' Yerucham Levovitz.

Story - R Moshe Feinstein, car ride, finger caught in door.

Leket Amorim Vol. 1 p 130-134 - *Kedushah* is giving, *tumah* is taking.

R' Yochanan Hasandler making a shoe to be the most durable and comfortable shoe possible.

Tehillim 92:10 - "יתפרדו כל פועלי און"

Gitin 56 - Titus's punishment, a gnat, can only take in, not give out.

• • •

Emissaries of Hashem - Giving is all gain

The president and the mugger.

Whose money is it anyway?

Story - Rav Yosef Shalom Elyashiv - you had all that money in your possession and you didn't use it to support *mosdos*?

Stories of *gedolim* who gave away packages of money without knowing the sum.

Shiluchei D'rachmanah - agents of Hashem to disperse his wealth.

Recent events indicate that a reassessment of our fiscal affixation is in order.

Mishlei 10:2 - "וצדקה תציל ממות" - as one of Hashem's *gabboim* of *tzedakah*.

Kiddushin 41 - שלוחו של אדם כמותו

In the את-בש *gematria*, צדקה is the equal of צדקה - one only gains from giving *tzedakah*.

• • •

Happy With His Portion - This above all else to thy own self be true

Irish fellows and dogs, bar, seeing-eye dog, a Chihuahua? That's what they gave me?

Avos 4:1 - "איזהו עשיר השמח בחלקו"

In our nonsensical yearning to be someone else, we lose sight of our unique task on this earth and squander our world in the process.

Sanhedrin 106 - The camel went to seek horns and not only didn't procure horn but his ears were cut off as well.

The *baal kinah* surrenders his entire raison d'etra for a tradeoff of futility

Sotah 9 - כל הנותן עיניו במה שאינו שלו מה שמבקש אין נותנים לו ומה שבידו נוטלין הימנו

The true *sameach b'chelko* is thrilled about his unique portion as well as his friend's unique portion.

Brachos 7 - כל הנהנה מסעודת חתן ואינו משמחו עובר בחמישה קולות

Kotzker, *Amud Ha'emes* p 135 - ואינו משמחו - refers to the guest himself.

• • •

Invisible - I feel your weight

Nurse, doctor, I can't see him right now.

Transparency and weightlessness, the silent treatment.

מפי מו״ר הרב שלמה) כבוד an expression of כָּבֵד, to feel the presence of others (פרייפלד).

Two powerful words - שלום עליכם

Yevamos 62 - the death of the *talmidim* of Rabi Akiva - מפני שלא נהגו כבוד זה לזה

Sanhedrin 20 - the greatest *dor* of Torah was the *dor* of Rabi Yehuda bar Ila'i - they learned Torah in great poverty.

Rabbi Chaim Shmuelevitz, *Sichos Mussar Maamar* 36 pg. 153 - ששה היו מתכסין בטלית א' and all were covered, their unusual sensitivity for one another made them the greatest *dor* of Torah.

Avos 3:3 - "שנים שיושבים ואין ביניהם... דברי תורה"
Kotzker, *Amud Ha'emes* p 163 - that is Torah.

Story - Chazon Ish walked in the street wearing his glasses.

• • •

Selflessness - The great prize of being a מעביר על מדותיו

Sara Finkel Mt. Sinai hospital.

Relinquishing for the sake of others.

Pesichtah D'Eichah Rabbasi - Rochel Imeinu not only gave Leah the *simanim*, but she hid underneath the bed and responded to Yaakov so as not to give away Leah's identity.

Rochel Imeinu's selflessness lies at the core of the power of her *tefillos* for her children עד היום הזה

Yirmiyahu 31:16-17 - "כה אמר ה' מנעי קולך מבכי ועיניך מדמעה כי יש שכר לפעולתך נאום ה' ושבו מארץ אויב ויש תקוה לאחריתך נאום ה' ושבו בנים לגבולם"

Shmuel II 1:26 - "נפלאתה אהבתך לי מאהבת נשים"

Harama Mipano (*Maamar Chakor, din* 4:17) - "מאהבת נשים" - the *ahavah* of Dovid and Yehonasan emanated from the *ahavah* of two famous women, Rochel and Leah.

Rosh Hashanah 17 - כל המעביר על מידותיו מוחלין לו על כל עוונותיו
Middah k'neged middah - if you let things pass, Hashem will let things pass.

A vilification can turn into a golden opportunity, a maligning, into a favorable circumstance.

Story - bar mitzvah, *leining*, two scheduled, one relinquished, hospital, Rav Elyashiv.

Taanis 22 - לעולם יהא אדם רך כקנה

• • •

That's His Problem - The staunch *emunah* of the עוסק בצרכי בצבור

Harry the worrier, that's his problem.

Not my problem, the courageous עוסקים בצרכי צבור.

Tefillas Mussaf- v'chol mi she'oskim bitzarchei tzibur b'emunah, what does it have to do with faith?

איתערותא דלעילא breeds איתערותא דלתתא

Bereishis 44:18 - "ויגש אליו יהודה"

The Gaon's *vort* – The *trup* explains why Yehuda the fourth son assumed this responsibility - קדמא ואזלא רביעי זרקא מנח סגול

Rabbi Shimon Schwab, *Maayan Bais Hashoevah* p 107 in the name of Rabbi Yosef Leib Bloch - the very *kabbalas achrayus* earned him a rush of energy and confidence.

Kuntres Meshiv Nefesh, perek 2:13 - Rabbi Chaim Shmuelevitz - the world says he who is *matzliach* is *b'simchah* when in fact it is he who is *b'simchah* who is *matzliach*.

Simchah, tzemichah (מפי מו"ר הרב שלמה פרייפעלד)

Tiferes Shlomo, Radamska Rebbe, *Parshas Re'eh* - רצון אותיות צנור - where there is a will, there is *siyatah d'Shmaya*.

By making our friend's problems ours, Hashem will make our problems "His".

• • •

We'll Leave the Light On For You - giving life to others

The man who thought he was a moth.

Bava Metziah 83 - עולם הזה דומה ללילה

Popular slogan - Motel 6 - we'll leave the light on for you.

People who suffer from a mood disorder precipitated by a lack of sunlight.

The greatness in being *b'simchah* and being *mesameach* others

Taanis 22 - הנך נמי בני עלמא דאתי נינהו אמר לה מאי עובדייכו אמרו ליה אינשי בדוחי אנן מבדחינן עציבי

Rashi ibid. - שמחים ומשמחים בני אדם

Bereishis 49:12 - "חכלילי עינים מיין ולבן שינים מחלב"

Kesubos 111 - אל תקרי ולבן שינים אלא ולבון שינים - the power of a smile

Shabbos 89 - משה אין שלום בעירך, היה לך לעזרני

Rashi ibid. - you should have said - תצלח במלאכתך

Kal v'chomer we should be *mechazek* one another and in doing so we imitate Hashem who is the quintessential *mechazek* and *mechayeh*.

Festivals

Elul-Teshuvah: How Will I Ever Get There? - A small step for man, a huge step for mankind

Sam late for work, I turned around to go home.

The difficulty of beginning the task at hand, especially one that is unpleasant.

Taanis 10 - *Tosfos divrei hamaschil p'siah* - כל התחלות קשות

Yeshayah 55:6 - "דרשו ה' בהמצאו"

Hashem beckons us to begin - "I'll help you!"

Midrash Tanchumah, Toldos 18 - פתחו לי פתח של תשובה כחודה של מחט ואני פותח לכם פתחים שיהיו עגלות וקרוניות נכנסות

Kotzker - Where is the *Ribono Shel Olam*? Wherever you let him in - מפי מו"ר הרב שלמה פריפלד

Maggid Mimezritch (*Leket Amorim* Vol. 2 p 44 brought in the *sefer* of the Imrei Pinchas *shaar* 2:117) - יש קונה עולמו בשעה אחת, *b'shaah* meaning with a (small) turn.

Bereishis 4:5 - "ואל קין ואל מנחתו לא שעה"

One small turn can last an eternity.

• • •

Sources and Outlines — 273

Rosh Hashanah-Teshuvah Return To Your Essence - Connecting to the G-dliness within.

Matt, the aspiring actor, hired in zoo to play an ape.

Chelek eloka m'maal - the beautiful *neshamah* ready to burst forth.

Sharei Teshuvah Shaar Harishon - מן הטובת אשר הטיב ה׳ עם ברואיו - *teshuvah*, one of the greatest gifts bestowed upon mankind.

Bava Metziah 21 - יאוש שלא מדעת - our worst enemy.

Giving up hope without even knowing what it's all about.

Yiush - the greatest area of decay today.

Maharal, *Derech Hachaim, Avos*- *perek* 1:2 *adam lashon m'od* - extended and expansive, the withering of the *tzuras ha'adam* מפי מו״ר הרב שלמה פרייפלד

Rambam, *Hilchos Teshuvah* 7:6 - *Gedolah teshuvah sh'mekareves es ha'adam laShechinah*, the process of *teshuvah* involves becoming *mekurav* once again to the *shechinah* within.

The concrete world, the abstract - *gashmiyus/ruchniyus*.

Tehillim 126:1 - ״בשוב ה׳ את שיבת ציון היינו כחולמים״.

Heard in the name of the Michtav M'Eliyahu - not ״נהיה כחולמים״, rather ״היינו כחולמים״ - we were always dreaming and viewed the physical world as concrete and the spiritual as abstract.

Eichah 5:21 - ״השיבנו ה׳ אליך״ - to the G-dliness within - ״ונשובה״ - and we will (inevitably) return (for this is the process of *teshuvah*).

• • •

Shabbos Shuvah-You Make Your Own Lunch - Yes you can; it's up to you

Mario and Antonio, tuna fish sandwich.

Shabbos shuvah - an auspicious moment when we must assume responsibility.

Avodah Zarah 17 - R' Elazar ben Durdaya, אין הדבר תלוי אלא בי , *yesh koneh olamo b'shaah achas.*

How can one do *teshuvah* in such a short time?

Teshuvah is a *d'var peleh* - one of the wonders of the world.

Teshuvah, hataras nedarim-(kol Nidrei)

Kiddushin 49 - *hamekadesh es ha'ishah al m'nas sh'ani tzaddik afilu rasha kol yamav mekudeshes* - שמא הרהר תשובה בדעתו - the amazing accomplishment of a pure moment

B'mefarshim ibid. - *safek mekudeshes.*

"כי המצוה הזאת... לא נפלאת היא ממך" - *Devarim* 30:11

Ramban ibid. - it refers to *teshuvah.*

How can *teshuvah* be described as not wondrous?

"לא נפלאת היא-ממך" of course *teshuvah* is miraculous but it is no more wondrous than you (are wondrous).

Nefesh Hachaim shaar aleph, perek 4 in the *hagah* - דע מה למעלה-ממך

Hoshea 14:2 - "שובה ישראל עד ה' אלוקיך"

• • •

Yom Kippur-Teshuvah-Coming Home - Rejoining the ranks of the *mamleches kohanim v'goy kadosh*

The diet, I'm 300 miles away from home.

A distorted view of *teshuvah* can lead to despondency.

Yoma 86 - *zedonos na'asos lo k'zochiyos*

Neshamah tehorah, nefesh beheimis.

Story - sign at Bronx Zoo - world's greatest predator, a mirror.

World view of man's potential - no more capable than a *beheimah*.

No *vidui* or *Al Cheit* on Rosh Hashanah the Yom Hadin, instead a heavy emphasis on *Malchus Shamayim*.

Only with the *romemus* that comes with the rejoining of the *Malchus Shamayim* on Rosh Hashanah can we face ourselves on Yom Kippur.

Shemos 19:6 - "ואתם תהיו לי ממלכת כהנים וגוי קדוש"

Tehillim 113:7-8 - "מקימי מעפר דל מאשפת ירים אביון להושיבי עם נדיבים עם נדיבי עמו"

• • •

Yom Kippur-Neilah-Teshuvah: Help Me Stop Stealing - Actualizing our full potetial

New Yorkers sharing a cab, battery and tires.

Although we are far from perfect, most of us are not thieves, yet, at *Neilah* there is no *Al Cheit*. Instead we say several times: למען נחדל מעושק ידינו - stop us from stealing

The *din* of Rosh Hashanah was on the day man was created, his *din* was one word "אַיֶּכָּה", what happened to you?

Chagigah 12 - Adam Harishon, *misof ha'olam v'ad sofo, min ha'aretz v'ad larakia.*

Adam, *ossiyos me'od* - stretchability

Midrash Simchah (Reb Simcha Bunim M'Pshis'cha) *Parshas Behar* - the *lifnim m'shuras hadin* of, "do not cheat your fellowman" is, "do not cheat yourself!"

Stop cheating yourself, stop short-changing your true potential, stop stealing!

אֵיכָה אותיות אַיֶּכָּה - the loss of the true dimensions of man is related to the destruction of the Bais Hamikdash

• • •

Sukkos-It's Time To Go Home - Under the shade and protection of the one above

Conversation between mother camel and baby camel, so why are we living in the San Diego zoo?

There's no place like home?

Diras keva/diras ara'i - תחת צילא דמהימנותא

Devarim 4:35 - "אין עוד מלבדו"

We are like a child cradled in its mother's arms, secure and trusting.

Metzudas Dovid Mishlei 15:30 - "כי אין בעולם שמחה כהתרת הספיקות" זמן שמחתינו

Amud Ha'emes (Kotzker) p 146 - מצטער פטור מן הסוכה - *shelo shayach l'mitzvas sukkah.*

Avodah Zarah 2 - the complaint of the *umos ha'olam l'asid lavo.*

Tehillim 27:4 - "שבתי בבית ה' כל ימי חיי לחזות בנועם ה' ולבקר בהיכלו" to live permanently with the same enthusiasm as one who visits from time to time.

• • •

Chanukah-Instant Kedushah - *kedushah* is attainable but not instantaneous

24/7 - not in a row.

The 24/7 convenience mindset of today's world.

Kabbalah for the layman - a twisted notion.

Mesillas Yesharim, perek 26 - ענין הקדושה תחילתה השתדלות וסופו מתנה

Yoma 39 - אדם מקדש עצמו מעט מקדשים אותו הרבה

Holiness in a world saturated with all that is impure.

Chullin 7 - ישראל קדושים הם - the purity and *lichtekeit* of a Jew in the darkest of times.

Pachad Yitzchak, Chanukah, *maamar* 3 - Chanukah, the last of the moadim.

Ne'os Hadesheh, Vol. 1 p 160 - the brazenness of the Yevanim, *azus d'kedushah.*

Ne'os Hadesheh, Chanukah Vol. 2 p 222 - lighting the menorah outside, below 10 *tefachim,* on the left side - in the face of the *kochos hatumah.*

Sukkah 5 - "לא ירדה שכינה למטה [מעשרה]"

Pachad Yitzchok, Chanukah, *maamar 3* - *shechichas haTorah* evolved into the rejuvenation of the Torah.

Menochos 99 - פעמים שביטולה של תורה זהו [קיומה] יסודה

Chanukah liturgy - אז אגמור שיר מזמור חנוכת המזבח

• • •

Purim-Everyone Should Enjoy Purim - The joy of basking in "His" glory

Tzu fil hollilus.

Celebrating Purim in a wild display of irresponsible inebriation debases the *chashivus* of one of the holiest days of the year.

Likutei haGr"a p 308, *Pachad Yitzchak*, Purim, *maamar 8* - Yom Kippur, Purim, *Chatzi laHashem, chatzi lachem.*

Megilah 7 - מיחייב איניש לבסומי בפוריא עד דלא ידע בין ארור המן לברוך מרדכי, since when is consuming alcoholic beverages a Jewish trait, let alone a mitzvah?

Rashi ibid. - להשתכר ביין the *lashon* of לבסומי בפוריא as opposed to לשכורי בחמרא בפוריא - to sweeten through Purim as opposed to becoming drunk with wine on Purim.

Ad d'lo yada? Basic *hashkafah* demands that we clearly discern between good and evil!

Taanis 29 - כשם שמשנכנס אב ממעטין בשמחה כך משנכנס אדר מרבים בשמחה - the relationship between Av and Adar.

The four *pesukim*, the *Megillas Esther* trup, the *Eichah* trup - major notes, minor notes.

Tekiyos d'meyushiv - the *tekiyos* that precede the *Mussaf Shemoneh Esrei* on Rosh Hashanah.

Tehillim 89:17 - "בשמך יגילון כל היום ובצדקתך ירומו" *roshei teivos b'chiyah* - the cry of a Jew is a cry of hope.

Shulchan Aruch, Orach Chaim 222:3 - חייב אדם לברך על הרע בדעת שלימה ובנפש חפצה כדרך שמברך בשמחה על הטובה כי הרעה לעובדי ה' היא שמחתם וטובתם כיון שמקבל מאהבה מה שגזר עליו ה' נמצא שבקבלת רעה זו הוא עובד את ה' שהיא שמחה לו

"כשם שמברכים על הטוב כך מברכים על הרע" - the amazing reversal of events on Purim allowed Klal Yisrael to see the טוב in the רע, come to full exposure.

Nesivos Shalom Purim - to become intoxicated with the revelation of Hashem's ever presence on Purim.

מו"ר הרב יעקב משה קולפסקי) is a *lashon* of, to sweeten the *din* ("לבסומי" בקונטרסו על פורים)

Ad d'lo yadah in the realm of *k'sheim sh'mevarchim*.

Story Merkaz HaRav, Ner Yaakov

"כי ה' הוא האלקים בשמים ממעל ועל הארץ מתחת אין עוד" - *Devarim* 4:39

• • •

Pesach-Freedom Of Religion - The freedom to actualize our *kochos haneshamah*

Israeli couple in bank, the prime minister's fault, you should see the line over there.

Defining our terms by their definitions, defining freedom as הפקרות.

"אין לך בן חורין אלא מי שעוסק בתלמוד תורה /אל תקרי חרות אלא חירות" - *Avos* 6:2
Ein lechah - no other definition.

Freedom is much more than just another word, it is an entire world and dimension with everything to gain.

"אדם לעמל יולד" - *Iyov* 5:7 - toiling in Torah to achieve freedom.
Becoming enslaved to their freedom.

"אנא ה' כי אני עבדך בן אמתך פתחת למוסרי" - *Tehillim* 116:16
How can these two concepts co-exist?

בראתי יצה"ר ובראתי לו תורה תבלין - *Kiddushin* 30

איזהו גבור הכובש את יצרו - *Avos* 4:1 - true freedom.

"הקנאה והתאוה והכבוד מוציאין את האדם מן העולם" - *Avos* 4:28 - controlling one's world through Torah.

"ואתם תהיו לי ממלכת כהנים וגוי קדוש" - *Shemos* 19:6

Mitzrayim *lashon meitzar* - the inescapable barrier of Mitzrayim.

• • •

Shavuos-Wheelbarrows - The *ikkar* is the *keili*

Russian factory, guard and comrade under suspicion, never caught, stealing wheelbarrows.

מניח את העיקר ותופס את הטפל, the *ikkar* is the *keili*.

Kedushas haz'man, oros hachag, the enormous opportunity it affords.

The Torah was given in a *midbar davka*, at Har Sinai, the lowest of the mountains, through Moshe Rabbeinu the most humble of men. *Bamidbar* 12:3 - "והאיש משה עניו מאד מכל האדם אשר על פני האדמה" *Midrash Aggadah Chukas* 21:19 - אין התורה מתקיימת אלא במי שעושה עצמו כמדבר

Siach Sarfei Kodesh - Gastona Rebbe - *milchigs* on Shavuos - because milk products spoil in fancy *keilim*, they stay fresh in simple *keilim*.

• • •

Tishah B'av-Tears Of Hope: Turn A Tear Into A Prayer - the crying of a Jew is one of hopefulness

B positive.

Story- Rav Yaakov Yosef Herman - dessert ordered, but not served, *zeicher l'churban*.

Story - Ribnitzer Rebbe wore sackcloth on Tishah B'Av.

Lamenting the length of *kinnos* more than the *churban habayis*.

Shemos 2:6 - "ותראהו את הילד והנה נער בוכה...ותאמר מילדי העברים זה"

Slonimer Rebbe - cry of a goy, cry of a *yid*, despair, hope.

Kinnos Tishah B'Av - "*sason v'simchah v'nas yagon va'anachah b'shuvi l'Yerushalayim*"

Brachos 10 - אפילו חרב חדה מונחת על צוארו של אדם אל ימנע עצמו מן הרחמים

The *kruvim* were embracing *b'sha'as hachurban*.

No *Tachanun* on Tishah B'Av.

Eichah 1:15 - "קרא עלי מועד"

When Hashem *k'veyachol* is without a home, He is even more accessible.

Eichah 1:3 - "כל רודפיה השיגוה בין המצרים"

Mashiach will be born on Tishah B'Av.

Expulsion of Jews from Spain on Tishah B'Av, Both WWI and WWII broke out on Tishah B'Av.

Twin Towers - 9/11(11th month, 9th day - 11/9 - Tishah B'Av - when counting from Tishrei)

The source - the *cheit hameraglim* - Tishah B'Av.

Taanis 29 - "Atem bachisem bechiyah shel chinam, v'ani koveiah lachem bechiyah l'doros"

Bechiyah shel chinam - the cry of a goy, the *tikkun* is a cry of hopefulness, the cry of a *yid*.

Tehillim 89:17 - "בשמך יגילון כל היום" - *roshei teivos bechiyah* (*seforim hakedoshim*), "kol hayom" even the most tragic of days.

Story - Rav Baruch Ber Leibovitz as a child when disciplined by his father turned a tear into a prayer.

Bereishis 18:14 - "היפלא מה' דבר?"

Internal Struggles

Compartmentalization: Light and Darkness All In One - The aggregate conflict in one man

The *shidduch* and the real mother-in-law.

The blatant contradictions in the behavior of mankind.

Melachim I 3:16-28 - The story of the two women who claimed the same baby as theirs.

Sichos Mussar maamar 12 p 49 - The amazing contradiction in the woman who said to kill the child.

Melachim I 13:4-6 - The story of Yeravam Ben Nevat, the *mizbeach*, and the Ish Ha'Elokim from Yehuda.

Ibid. 13:4 - "וישלח ירבעם את ידו מעל המזבח לאמר תפסוהו"

Ibid. 13:6 – "ויען המלך ויאמר אל איש האלקים חל נא את פני ה' אלקך והתפלל בעדי ותשב ידי אלי ויחל איש האלקים את פני ה' ותשב יד המלך אליו ותהי כבראשנה"

Rashi in *Mishlei* - "V'tehi k'varishonah" - *Omeid umaktir la'avodas gilulim ve'af besof kein.*

Birchas Krias Shema - *Yotzer or u'vorei choshech*, light and darkness are independent of one another.

Kiddushin 30 - למיימינין בה סמא דחיי למשמאילין בה סמא דמותא - even Torah can be twisted and distorted by virtue of the inherent contradictions in man.

Attacking on two fronts with the hope that a little light diffuses a lot of darkness.

• • •

Enemies in the West - Dealing with Eisav when he acts as your brother

The knight reporting on the war effort.

The naivety in thinking that Jews who enjoy freedom are devoid of enemies in western culture.

Acceptance and tolerance is appreciated, yet can be our greatest enemy.

The spiritual holocaust of assimilation.

Bereishis 32:12 - "הצילני נא מיד אחי מיד עשו" - when Eisav acts as our brother there is even greater concern.

The world of Eisav as our brother is the world of tremendous *yetzer hara*. How are we to deal with it?

Kiddushin 30 - בראתי יצר הרע ובראתי לו תורה תבלין

The *refuah* always precedes the *makkah*.

The literal translation of *tavlin* is spice, not remedy.
Torah does not remedy the *yetzer hara*. It channels its *koach*.

Chessed meaning kindness, chessed meaning shame.

Vayikrah 20:17 - "ואיש אשר יקח את אחתו בת אביו או בת אמו וראה את ערותה והיא תראה את ערותו חסד הוא ונכרתו לעיני בני עמם ערות אחתו גלה עונו ישא"

Channelization in avodas Hashem.

Our power to channel the forces of evil is a yerushah from Yaakov Avinu in his victory over the Saro shel Eisav.

"ישראלי" b'gematria 541 = 182 "יעקב" plus 359 "שטן", representing Yisrael's power to channel the kochos of the Satan.

Midrash Shir Hashirm - ישראל - an acronym for יש ששים רבוא אותיות לתורה

• • •

Here Today, Gone Tomorrow - Becoming an accomplice to the yetzer hara

Is that all you people ever think about?

The power of the yetzer hara is in small increments (a little at a time.)

Shabbos 105 - Kach umnaso shel yetzer hara. Hayom omer lo asei kach ul'machar omer lo asei kach ad sh'omer lo leich avod avodah zarah.

Shemos 15:2 - "זה קלי ואנוהו"

Eigel hazahav a case at point.

Shemos 32:8 - "סרו מהר מין הדרך אשר צויתים עשו להם עגל מסכה"

How could it happen so quickly?

Tricked by the Satan, he showed them the mitah shel Moshe, the sky blackened, despair and despondency enveloped them, then the Satan is empowered to make big gains.

Sichos Mussar, maamar 55 p 234 - When despondent even a dor de'ah can be quickly transformed into idol worshippers.

Ramban, Bereishis 4:3 - Kayin was the first to understand the sod of korbonos.

Targum Yonoson, Bereishis 4:8 - "In a fit of anger he went from an oved Hashem to a kofer b'ikkar, declaring "leis din v'leis dayan!"

Such is the power of the *yetzer* over one who is angry.

• • •

Who Is Like You, Hashem! - You even sustain the rebel

Shidduch, the Ribono Shel Olam will help, he thinks that I'm the Ribono Shel Olam.

Devarim 28:9 - "והלכת בדרכיו"

Shabbos 133 - "Mah Hu chanun v'rachum af atah heyei chanun v'rachum", although we strive to emulate Hashem, we know that we are far from his equal.

Sefer Tomer Devorah describes the 13 *middos* of Hashem and explains how we can model our lives after them.

Michah 7:18-20 - the source of those *middos*.

Yeshaya 14:14 - "אעלה על במתי עב אֲדַמֶה לעליון"

Shelah Hakadosh p 3a, 20b - "Adam" lashon "adameh"

Michah 7:18 - "מי קל כמוך" - even the sinner is included in G-d's graciousness, a thought that should humble the most hardened criminal.

Brachos 54 - "בכל לבבך" – *b'shnei yetzarechah*, serve Hashem with your *yetzer hara* by invoking this awe inspiring thought that even as I rebel, Hashem still sustains me.

Story - Rav Yaakov Yitzchak Ruderman, Rav Michoel Forshlager, and my father, Rav Yaakov Kurland, "learn Torah with your *yetzer hara*."

Hashem created everything in existence with the potential to be used as a medium to serve him; even the *yetzer hara*.

Spiritual Tools

Man's True Strength - Uniting the forces of one's heart

The Sahara Forest.

A world obsessed with physical prowess, has stripped man of his true strength.

Maharal Derech Chaim 1:2 - "adam" - "me'od" stretchability.

Ein davar ha'omed bifnei haratzon - מו״ר הרב שלמה פרייפלד

Sanhedrin 38 - The original *tzuras ha'adam* - Adam Harishon, *misof haolam ad sofo, min ha'aretz ad la'rakia*.

Sichos Mussar, maamar 32 p 135 - Bas Pharaoh's hand extending to reach the basket not a *neis*, but a result of pure *ratzon*.

Piyut for *Tefillas Geshem* – "*Yichad leiv v'gal even m'pi be'er mayim*" (regarding Yaakov Avinu removing the rock from well).

Sichos Mussar ibid. - *Yichud haleiv* - the uniting of the forces of one's heart results in the transcending of the limitations of nature.

Tehillim 68:35 - "תנו עוז לאלקים״

Nefesh Hachaim shaar aleph perek dalet – ואל יאמר בלבו חי״ו כי מה אני ומה כחי לפעול במעשי השפלים שום ענין בעולם (אלא) שכל א׳ מן המעשים עולה כפי שרשה לפעול פעולתה בגבהי מרומים וכו׳

Avos 2:1 - ״דע מה למעלה ממך עין רואה ואזן שומעת וכל מעשיך בספר נכתבין״
Nefesh Hachaim ibid. – דע מה למעלה ממך, כל מה שנעשה בעולמות העליונים גבוהי גבוהים הכל ממך, everything that occurs above is through your actions below.

Sanhedrin 37 - בשבילי נברא העולם - my contribution counts in a big way.

Birchos Krias Shema – ״ויחד לבבנו לאהבה וליראה את שמך ולא נבוש לעולם ועד״

• • •

Not So Fast - The pros and cons of adaptation

The drill sergeant, not so fast Goldberg.

The contrast between Avraham Avinu and Sarah Imeinu in their response to the news of the *akeidah*.

Bereishis 22:2 - ״קח נא את בנך את יחידך אשר אהבת את יצחק״
Rashi ibid. - את בנך אמר לו שני בנים יש לי את יחידך אמר לו זה יחיד לאמו וזה יחיד לאמו אשר אהבת אמר לו שניהם אני אוהב את יצחק שלא לערבבו פתאום ותזוח דעתו עליו ותטרף
Rashi ibid. - פרחה נשמתה ממנה ומתה

Yoma 77 - אין משיבין על הקלקלה - not to be the bearer of bad news, incremental absorption allows for adaptation.

Man's ability to adapt can diffuse inspiration (*regilus*).

Yechezkel 46:9 – "והבא דרך שער צפון להשתחות יצא דרך שער נגב והבא דרך שער נגב יצא דרך שער צפונה לא ישוב דרך השער אשר בא בו כי נכחו יצא"

Hachossid Yaavatz, Avos 1:4 - In order to avoid allowing familiarity to breed comfortability which can suffocate inspiration.

Sanhedrin 19 - פלטי שמו ולמה נקרא פלטיאל שפלטו קל מן העבירה

The *machlokes* between Shaul and Dovid regarding the status of Paltiel's new wife.

Sanhedrin ibid. - כל העוסק בדבר זה ידקר בחרב זה

Sichos Mussar, maamar 11 p 46 - How did Paltiel's action protect him when he could so easily remove that sword? It served as a perpetual remainder that there had been a time when he felt so strong about this separation and could thereby revert back to that moment of inspiration.

Shir Hashirim 3:5 - "אם תעירו ואם תעוררו את האהבה עד שתחפץ"

Ramban, Shir Hashirim - "עד שתחפץ" a *lashon* of a *chefetz*, transpose the inspiration into a physical object (heard from מו"ר הרב נפתלי יגר)

Paltiel's genius in fighting the malaise of *regilus* (adaptation).

• • •

To Tell The Truth - Unflinching commitment to integrity

Two elderly gentlemen with the same foot ailment, do you think I showed the doctor the right foot?

Submerged in a world of *sheker*, it is difficult to be *modeh al ha'emes*.

Shabbos 55 - Chosamo shel Hakodosh Baruch Hu emes (*tzaddikim* emulate Hashem's *middah* of *emes*)

Chulin 91 - צדיקים חביבים עליהם ממונם יותר מגופם (because of the integrity that went into its acquisition).

Story - Chiddushei Harim, Rav Akiva Eiger, Rav Yaakov M'Lisa and the Chemdas Shlomo (as heard מפי מו"ר הרב שלמה פרייפלד)
ועי' בספר מאיר עיני הגולה עמוד כ"ז \ קע"ד סיפור דומה קצת לזה

Story - Rav Yaakov Kaminetsky and eating *gebokts*.

Story - Rav Aharon Kotler and the yeshiva stationary.

Story - Crazy man driving down the boulevard the wrong way.

Story - 9th grade English teacher, never wrong.

In a world of state-of-the-art perfection, it is difficult to admit imperfection.

In a throw away society why make the attempt to fix things by admitting one's mistakes

Story - Man in Los Angeles with watch that ran three hours fast.

The *cheit ha'egel* was forgiven, the *cheit hameraglim* was not.

Baal Shem Tov al HaTorah, Parshas shelach - in the *cheit ha'egel*, they were *modeh al ha'emes*, in the *cheit hameraglim*, they were not.

"וישב משה אל ה' ויאמר אנא חטא העם הזה חטאה גדולה" - *Shemos* 32:31

"הננו ועלינו אל המקום אשר אמר ה' כי חטאנו" - *Bamidbar* 14:40

Story - *Kabbalah* of *kehillah* stricken with many anti-Semitic decrees to accept all reproach for thirty days without a response or defense.

Shalom Bayis-The Home

Home Sweet Home - *Midos tovos* and *eidelkeit* begin at home.

The absent-minded professor.

The anomaly of the *baal middos* in public and raving madman at home.

We hurt those closest to us and inevitably teach our children to do the same.

Human nature, perhaps, but unacceptable for a *Torahdike* Jew.

Brachos 28 - Rav Yochonan Ben Zakkai's *brachah* to his *talmidim* on his deathbed "עד כאן?" they asked, "יהי רצון שתהא מורא שמים עליכם כמורא בשר ודם" To which he answered, "ולואי, תדעו כשאדם עובר עבירה אומר שלא יראני אדם"

The *Ribono shel Olam* is the מקומו של עולם , at home we feel we can "be ourselves," Hashem *yerachem*, there is no privacy that excludes the *Ribono shel Olam*, certainly not the very home that we endeavor to transform into a comfortable abode for the *Shechinah*.

• • •

Sailing The Seven C's Of Chinuch - Seven rules to follow in *chinuch habanim*.

The heretical Hebrew school teacher and the precocious child.

1. Conduct - the way we conduct our lives will be absorbed by osmosis.

2. Cognizance - appreciating the greatness of the gift of children in a self-serving world.

Nedarim 54 - "*Arba'ah chashuvim k'mais v'echad meihem mi sh'ain lo banim.*"

3. Cuddling - showering our children with love and affection.

4. C(k)avod - *Sefer Atarah Lamelech* (Harav Avraham Pam) p 89 - לבייש אדם מישראל הוא איסור לאו דאורייתא וכו' וזה כולל גם קטנים...ואפשר להשפיע יותר בדרכי כבוד ונועם

A child is a person with real feelings and they must feel our respect for them. In doing so, we teach them the greatest lesson in *kibbud av v'aim*.

5. Consolation - we must develop a rapport with our children so that they feel our unlimited friendship and listening ear.

Avos 5:25 - בן שמונה עשרה לחופה

6. Crisis management-riding out the storm and keeping the lines of communication open.

7. C(s)iyata d'Shmaya-we must *daven*.

• • •

The Bar Mitzvah-The Bar Chiyuvah - The privilege of serving the master and adhering to his decrees

Reform rabbi rids the temple of its rodents.

What happened to that kid with the squeaky voice?

Kiddushin 31 - the source for a seudas bar mitzvah.

Kiddushin ibid. - גדול המצווה ועושה יותר ממי שאינו מצווה ועושה.

Joining the ranks of those who perform mitzvos because they are gezeiros haMelech is worthy of יומא טבא לרבנן

Brachos 33 - "האומר על קן צפור יגיעו רחמיך משתקין אותו"

בגמ׳ שם-מפני שעושה מדותיו של הקב״ה רחמים ואינן אלא גזירות

ע״ש פי׳ רש״י-והוא לא לרחמים עשה אלא להטיל על ישראל חקי גזירותיו להודיע שהם עבדיו ושומרי מצוותיו וגזירות חוקותיו אף בדברים שיש לשטן לעכו״ים להשיב עליהם ולומר מה צורך במצוה זו

Story - Rav Yaakov Kurland's derashah at his grandson Chaim's bar mitzvah shortly after September,. 11, 2001 - today the whole world has become a *bar chiyuvah*.

We should draw strength from the freshness of the new *bar chiyuvah*.

Tefillah

Keep On "Shuckling" - קוה אל ה׳ חזק ויאמץ לבך וקוה אל ה׳

Bugzie Goldberg, it was the best I could do under the circumstances.

Brachos 10 - אפילו חרב חדה מונחת על צוארו של אדם אל ימנע עצמו מן הרחמים

Bereishis 24:63 - "ויצא יצחק לשוח בשדה"

Brachos 26 - ואין שיחה אלא תפלה

שיח בגימטריא 318, יאוש בגימטריא 317

Story - Ponevitzer Rav, Hashem is definitely listening, but for now, the answer is no.

Tefillos are never wasted, one *shleps* in the other.

Devarim 4:23 - ואתחנן בגימטריא 515, Moshe davened 515 tefillos to be allowed entry into the land.

Brachos 10 - Chizkiyahu Hamelech and Yeshayah Hanavi, "כלא נבואתך וצא"

The realm of *tevah* and *nissim* are one marvelous providential domain.

Birchas Krias Shema - "מחדש בכל יום תמיד מעשה בראשית"

אלקים בגימטריא הטבע-86 (*Leket Amorim* vol. 1)

Bereishis 18:14 - "היפלא מה' דבר"

Tehillim 35:10 - "כל עצמותי תאמרנה ה' מי כמוך"

• • •

Tefillah: It's Not Just Three Times a Day - Tefillah, 24/7 - חיי שעה

The parking spot.

Secular view of prayer; for emergency situations.

Tefillah, just three times a day, is also a misunderstanding of its true essence.

Shabbos 10. Tefillah - חיי שעה, Torah - חיי עולם.

Brachos 6 - Tefilah is described as דברים העומדים ברומו של עולם ובני אדם מזלזלין בהן

Shulchan Aruch, Orach Chaim 98:1 - through *tefillah* one can soar to heights close to prophecy.

Yeshaya 1:18 - "לכו נא ונוכחה יאמר ה'" *tefillah* as an ongoing dialogue with Hashem.

Bereishis 24:63 - "ויצא יצחק לשוח בשדה"

Brachos 26 - אין שיחה אלא תפלה - conversing is the very nucleus of *tefillah*.

Story - Bubby Rissel Zelman zt"l - "Hashem is my friend. I speak to him."

Mesillas Yesharim, perek 19 - אמנם מי שהוא בעל שכל נכון במעט התבוננות ושימת לב יוכל לקבוע בלבו אמיתת הדבר איך הוא בא ונושא ונותן ממש עמו יתברך ולפניו הוא מתחנן ומאתו הוא מבקש והוא יתברך שמו מאזין לו מקשיב לדבריו כאשר ידבר איש לרעיהו ורעיהו מקשיב ושומע אליו"

Brachos 28 - העושה תפילתו קבע אין תפילתו תחנונים - the prayer of rote performance has no appeal.

The וכוח of *tefillah* helps the *mispalel* clarify his priorities.

Tefillah is called חיי שעה because it is in fact available 24/7, non-stop.

The World We Live In

Deadheads - The precious moments of real living

Steve meets an old man in the cemetery, if I was alive I'd be scared to!

A society replete with deadheads-the living dead.

Brachos 18 - אלו רשעים שבחייהם קרוים מתים

Brachos 18 - צדיקים במיתתם נקראו חיים ק"ו בחייהם

Bereishis 24:1 – "ואברהם זקן בא בימים"

Rashi ibid. - כל ימיו אתו

Bereishis 23:1 – "ויהיו חיי שרה מאה שנה ועשרים שנה ושבע שנים שני חיי שרה"

Rashi ibid. - כולן שוין לטובה

Sichos Mussar 92 p 392 - Avraham and Sarah shared a common outlook on life that every treasured moment was a potential brick to build upon yet another, in constructing a world edifice.

עשו lashon עשוי, already done, אדום lashon דממה, silent and lifeless.

Bereishis 25:25 – "כולו כאדרת שער" - born fully matured, no longer growing.

Bereishis 25:27 – "איש שדה" - *Targum Onkelos* - גבר נחשירכן which means נח ובטל (*Tosfos, Bava Kamah* 92)

Bereishis 25:27 – "ויעקב איש תם יושב אהלים"

Targam Yonoson Ben Uziel ibid. - תבע אולפין - one who pursues greatness, full of vitality, vision and purpose.

Bereishis 47:28 – "ויחי יעקב" - Yaakov Avinu's demise is expressed with the words, "and he lived."

Taanis 5 - יעקב אבינו לא מת

• • •

Life Insurance - The secret to longevity

An eighty year old man purchases life insurance.

Mankind's pre-occupation with extending life, dreaming the impossible dream.

A *yid* views the world from spectacles of eternity in a structured program of Torah and *mitzvos* that allow him to live forever.

Birchos Krias Shemah shel Arvis - "כי הם חיינו וארך ימינו"

Torah

Never The Same - (The Same Thing Syndrome) - Real learning-constant review

Abe Schwartz, the proprietor of the local Chinese laundry.

Shabbos 127 - ותלמוד תורה כנגד כולם

The importance of *chazarah* as the mainstay of the fulfillment of this important mitzvah.

The same thing syndrome - it's old hat, I've done that, been there.

Devarim 11:13 - "והיה אם שמע תשמעו"

Brachos 40 - אם שמוע בישן תשמע בחדש

Kinyan haTorah is the *ikkar*.

Kiddushin 32 - בסוגיא של רב שמחל על כבודו, כבודו מחול או אין כבודו מחול

Tehillim 1:2 - "כי אם בתורת ה' חפצו ובתורתו יהגה יומם ולילה"

Rashi, *Kiddushin* 32 - at first it is Hashem's Torah but, משלמדה וגרסה , it is called his own.

Brachos 6 - אגרא דפרקא רהטא shouldn't the primary reward be because of the learning itself?

Rashi ibid. - שהרי רובם אינם מבינים להעמיד גירסא ולומר שמועה מפי רבן לאחר זמן שיקבלו שכר למוד

Brachos 32 - regarding the *chassidim harishonim* - תורתן היאך משתמרת

Maharsha ibid. - וזה החסיד ששוהה ביום ט' שעות בתפלה אין לו זמן לחזור על התורה

Purim and Chanukah, the two *yomim tovim d'rabanan*, bridge the gap until the coming of Mashiach.

Each has an element of *kabalas haTorah*.

Shabbos 88 - הדר קבלוה בימי אחשורוש

Shabbos 21 - מאי חנוכה דתנו רבנן, the *pilpulah shel Torah* that followed the *shechichas haTorah* brought about by the Yevanim.

Chiddushei Harim al Hatorah (Chanukah) - מאי חנוכה-what is the essence of Chanukah? דתנו רבנן - the perpetuation of Klal Yisrael through the *pilpulah shel Torah* of *Torah Shebaal peh*.

Pachad Yitzchak, Chanukah, *maamar* 3- פעמים שביטולה של תורה זו היא קיומה

Shabbos 21 - *Mehadrin min hamehadrin*.

P'nei Yehoshua, Shabbos 21 - Why did they require a *neis*; והלא טומאה הותרה בצבור

Beis Halevi al HaTorah, Chanukah- why did they require a *neis*; והלא אין שיעור לעובי הפתילות

The *neis* of Chanukah came about because of their insistence in being *mehader b'mitzvos*.

The מצוה הידור of *limud haTorah* is constant *chazarah*.

The expression of הדר קבלוהו בימי אחשורוש, an expression of הדר meaning returning, reviewing - חזרה - from the *ahavas haneis* they accepted to learn Torah with a commitment to make it theirs forever.

• • •

The "Chein" of the Plain and the Humble - "ולענווים יתן חן"

Harvey and the hot bath.

Shabbos 31 - Hillel Hazakein's great patience in the face of an obnoxious questioner.

Ibid. - "לעולם יהא אדם ענוותן כהלל" - the underlying secret, his great humility.

Teshuvos Rabi Akiva Eiger in the *hakdamah*

Story of Rav Moshe Feinstein, translating neighbor's letters from the Russian language.

Mishlei 3:34 - "ולענווים יתן חן"

Mishlei 1:9 - "כי לוית חן הם לראשך וענקים לגרגרתך"

The fusion of simplistic greatness of *talmidei chachamim*.

Avos 1:4 והוה מתאבק בעפר רגליהם

• • •

Turn A Shiur Into A Prayer - *Limud haTorah*, an exercise in *deveikus*

Seymour didn't purchase a seat in shul for the high holidays.

Learning Torah as a prayer, becoming familiar with the vernacular of Hashem.

Brachos 21 - *Birchas haTorah* before learning Torah - "כי שם ה' אקרא הבו גודל לאלקינו"

Maharshah ibid. - The Torah is a conglomerate of many combinations of the names of Hashem.

Rav Tzadok Hakohein, *Tzidkas Hatzadik* 182 - The study of Torah is called calling out to Hashem.

Tehillim 119:62 - "חצות לילה אקום להודת לך על משפטי צדקך"

Tehillim 119:147 - "קדמתי בנשף ואשועה"

Brachos 3 - עד חצות הלילה היה עוסק בדברי תורה מכאן ואילך בשירות ותשבחות

Sh'arim B'tefillah - שעוה סוג של תפלה, learning Torah is called praying.

Tehillim 19:8 - "תורת ה' תמימה משיבת נפש"

Shmuel I 1:15 - "ואשפוך את נפשי לפני ה'" - *nefesh lashon tefillah*, "*m'shivas nefesh*," a communication of *tefillah*.

Brachos 8 - מיום שחרב בית המקדש אין לו להקב"ה בעולמו אלא ד' אמות של הלכה בלבד

Avos 5:26 - "הפך בה הפך בה כולה בה"

Glossary

(al) Kiddush Hashem: (in) sanctification of G-d's name

Adam: The first man, Humanity

Ahava, (Ahavas): Love (of)

Aibishter: Lit. The most high one (G-d) (Yiddish)

Al Cheit: Lit. On the sin. A longer confession, with full sentences expressing regret for each of a number of sins

Amah (Amos): Cubit, Biblical and halachic unit of measurement of about 18-24 inches

Ashamnu: Lit. We have sinned, A short confession enumerating an alphabetical list of 24 sins.

Baal Korei: Torah reader

Ba'alei Madreigah: Lit. Masters of levels, People of spiritual accomplishment

Bachur: Youth, Yeshivah student

Bamidbar: Numbers

Beis medrash: Study hall

Ben: The son of

Bentch: To bless, To recite the Grace after a meal

Bentcher: A book that contains traditional blessings, primarily the Grace After Meals

Bereishis: Genesis

Birchas Hatorah: The blessing that relates to the study of Torah

Birchas Kohanim: The tradition blessing of the congregation by the Kohanim

Bitachon: Faith, Trust

Blatt: Two sided page

Bnei Torah: Children (i.e. followers) of the Torah

Bris: Circumcision

Chalav Yisrael: Milk that has been produced under the supervision of a Jew

Chashivus: Importance

Chashuv: Distinguished, Noteworthy

Chassan: Bridegroom, Betrothed

Chassan Torah, Chassan Bereishis: Synagogue honor on the day of Simchas Torah

Chazal; Abbr. Chachameinu Zichronam Livracha: Our wise men, may their memory be blessed. Used mainly for Misnaic and Talmudic sages.

Chessed: Kindness

Chinuch: Education, Inauguration

Chuppah: (Marriage) canopy

Darshan: Interpret, often homiletically

Daven: Pray

Devarim: Deuteronomy

Divrei Hayamim: The Book of Chronicles

Dor De'ah: Knowledgeable generation

Drasha: (Homiletical) interpretation

Ehrlich: Upstanding

Eichah: The Book of Lamentations

Elokim: G-d

Emes: Truth

Emunah: Trust, Faith

Ga'avah: Haughtiness

Gadol, (gedolim): Great (sage[s])

Galus: Exile, Diaspora

Gaon: Genius

Geshmak: Enjoyable (Yiddish)

Gut: Good (Yiddish)

Hakadosh Baruch Hu: The Holy One, Blessed is He

Halachos: Torah laws

Har Sinai: Mt. Sinai, site where the Torah was given to Israel

Hartzig: Heartfelt (Yiddish)

Hashkafah: Outlook, Weltanschauung

Hataras Nedarim: Absolution of Vows (A legal concept, as well as a traditional Rosh Hashanah repentance ceremony)

Hy"d; abbr. Hashem yinkom damo: May G-d avenge his death

Ishah Hashunamis: Woman from Shunam

Iyov: The Book of Job

Kabbalah: Hidden and esoteric portion of the Torah

Kabbalas haTorah: Acceptance of the Torah

Kal V'chomer: A fortiori; a logical proof of "greater certainty"

Kavod: Honor, Respect

Kedoshim: Martyrs

Kedushah: Holiness

Kibbud av v'eim: (The commandment of) honoring one's parents

Kishka: Stuffed intestine with a filling made from a combination of meat and grain

Koach (kochos): Strength, Ability, Potential

Kofer: Denier (of G-d)

Koheles: Ecclesiastes

Kohen, (Kohanim): Priests, during the days of the Temple; kohanim today are their descendants

Kol Nidrei: Lit. all vows. Prayer said on the commencement of Yom Kippur

Lashon Hara: Lit. Evil tongue, Gossip

Lein: Read, usually from the Torah in the synagogue (Yiddish)

Limud: Study, Learning

Litvishe: Lithuanian (Yiddish)

Ma'avir sedrah: To review the week's Torah portion

Ma'oz Tzur: Traditional Chanukah hymn

Mashgiach: Spiritual supervisor in a Yeshivah

Mechanech: Educate (educator), Inaugurate

Megillas Esther: The Book of Esther

Melachim: The Book of Kings

Melaveh malka: Lit. Escort the queen, Meal eaten shortly after Shabbos

Mesiras nefesh: Willingness to forfeit oneself

middah k'neged middah: Measure for measure

Middah, Middos: Personality trait(s) tendency(ies)

Minyan: Quorum of ten required for prayer, Gathering of ten for the purpose of prayer

Mishlei: The Book of Proverbs

Misnaged (Misnagdim): Lit. Opposer(s), people who are not chassidic.

Mitzvah (mitzvos): Good deed(s)

Mizbe'ach: Altar (of the Holy Temple)

Mussaf: Additional prayer of Shabbos and Yom Tov

Mussar: Lit. rebuke, The practice of introspective self improvement

Nachas: Appreciation, usually of a child by a parent or mentor

Nasi: Leader of Klal Yisrael during mishnaic period

Navi: Prophet

Ne'ilah: The closing prayer of Yom Kippur

Neshamah, Neshamos: Soul(s)

Nisayon: Challenge, Test

Oved: Servant of

Parnassah: Livelihood, Sustenance

Parshah: Weekly Torah Portion

Passuk (pesukim): Verse(s)

R"l Abbr. Rachmana Litzlan: May G-d protect us

Rasha: A wicked, sinful and/or evil person

Rav: Rabbi, Sage

Rebbi: Spiritual teacher

Ribono Shel Olam: Master of the World

Rosh yeshiva: Head of a Yeshivah

Ruach Hakodesh: G-dly inspiration

Schmaltz: Fat (Yiddish)

Seder: 1.Scheduled study session 2. Traditional Pesach meal

Sefarim: (Holy) Books

Shalom: Peace

Shalom aleichem: Peace unto you, (traditional greeting)

Shalosh Seudos: Lit. Three meals, The third meal of Shabbos

Shas: The Talmud

Shechinah: Divine Presence

Shemos: Exodus

Shidduch: Potential marriage partner

Shir Hashirim: The Song of Songs

Shlep: Lug, Drag, Tote (Yiddish)

Shlit"a; abbr. sheyichyeh l'yamim tovim aruchim: May he live long and be well

Shmooze: Chat

Shmuel: The Book of Samuel

Shofar: Ram's horn

Shoftim: The Book of Judges

Shoresh: Essence, Root

Shuckel: Sway back and forth

Shulchan Aruch: Major code of Jewish law

Simchah: Joy

Siyata Dishmaya: Help of Heaven (Aramaic)

Sugya: Topic in the Talmud

Ta'avah: Desire, Temptation

Talmid: Student

Talmid Chacham: Torah scholar

Tanna: Rabbinic scholar cited in the Mishnah

Tefach (tefachim): Handbreadth

Tefilla (Tefillos): Prayer(s)

Tehillim: The Book of Psalms

Tekiya (Tekiyos): Blast(s) of the Shofar

Teshuvah: Repentance, Penance, Return

Torah Sheba'al Peh: Oral Torah, i.e Talmud and Medrash as opposed to The Bible

Trei Asar: The Twelve Prophets

Trup: Cantillation, Notation for chanting of Torah reading

Tzaddik, (tzaddikim): Righteous person (people)

Tzadekes: Righteous woman

Tzedakah: Charity

Tzelem: Form, Shape

Tzinim Pachim: Chills and fevers

Tzu kumt mir: I deserve it (Yiddish)

Vayikra: Leviticus

Vort: Lit. Word, usually used for a novel interpretation of Torah

Yechezkel: The Book of Ezekiel

Yeherag v'al ya'avor: Prohibitions for which one must choose death over transgression

Yehoshua: The Book of Joshua

Yeshayahu: The Book of Isaiah

Yeshuah, (Yeshuos): Salvations(s)

Yetzer Hara: Evil Inclination, Temptation

Yetzer Tov: Inclination towards good

Yid, (Yidden): Jew(s) (Yiddish)

Yiras Shamayim: Fear of Heaven

Yirmiyahu: The Book of Jeremiah

Yom Tov (Yamim Tovim): Jewish holidays

Zemer, (Zemiros): Song(s)

Zocheh: Merit, Be privileged

Zt"l: abbr. of Zichrono Tzaddik Livracha: The memory of righteous people is a blessing